DRUGS DECISIONS:

A QUALITATIVE STUDY
OF YOUNG PEOPLE

THE UNIVERSITY

DRUGS DECISIONS:
A QUALITATIVE STUDY
OF YOUNG PEOPLE

Annabel Boys, Jane Fountain, John Marsden, Paul Griffiths,
Garry Stillwell and John Strang
National Addiction Centre, Institute of Psychiatry

HEA Project Team
Joan Heuston
Senior Research Manager
Ann McNeill
Strategic Research Adviser

21284180

The views expressed in this report are those of
the authors and not necessarily those of the HEA.

ISBN 0 7521 1591 X

Health Education Authority
Trevelyan House
30 Great Peter Street
London SW1P 2HW

www.hea.org.uk

Text composition Ken Brooks
Printed in Great Britain

CONTENTS

ACKNOWLEDGEMENTS

The authors wish to acknowledge the support of Joan Heuston and Ann McNeill of the Health Education Authority.

Several organisations were very helpful in assisting with the recruitment of young people for the study. In order to maintain confidentiality, these cannot be named, but their collaboration was very much appreciated.

We also thank colleagues at the National Addiction Centre who assisted with the project.

Finally, thanks are especially due to the young people who gave so generously of their time and trust to participate in the study.

FOREWORD

In the last couple of decades increasing numbers of young people have been experimenting with a variety of drugs. At present, little is known about the processes that influence a young person's decisions with respect to their drug use. In order to understand some of these decisions-making factors the Health Education Authority (HEA), as part of its exploratory and developmental research work, commissioned this small-scale study.

Our aim was to investigate how a sample of young people aged 16–21 decide whether or not to use a range of illicit drugs or alcohol, and the factors that influence these choices. The research examines the reasons for the selection of particular drugs and reports how different drugs serve different functions for the consumer.

The study forms part of the HEA's overall research strategy and the findings, although preliminary, should help to inform further research in this important area and contribute to the development of new education and prevention initiatives.

Joan Heuston
Ann McNeill
Una Canning
HEA Research Directorate

LIST OF TABLES

EXECUTIVE SUMMARY

Purpose

This report presents the key findings from a qualitative study of 50 young people aged 16–21. The primary purpose of the study was to identify factors which influence the decisions young people make about using drugs and alcohol. In this context decision-making spans a variety of topics, such as whether to experiment with illicit drugs, which of a range of available substances to use, the size of doses and chosen limits, and so on.

The study was conceived as a small-scale investigation which would also serve to inform the planning of further research in this arena.

Little is known about the decision-making processes which underlie young people's use of psychoactive substances. Knowledge of the reasons for the selection of particular drugs and the functions these serve can inform the future development of effective material for new education and prevention programmes.

Recruitment

Interviews were conducted during 1997. A small sample of young people in the target age range were sought from a wide range of social and economic backgrounds, levels of education and current occupations. A snowballing recruitment method was used with seven starting points. A central inclusion criterion for participation in the study was lifetime use of at least one of the following substances: alcohol, cannabis, amphetamines, ecstasy or LSD.

As we did not aim to obtain a representative sample, no inferences are made relating to the behaviour or experiences of young people in the UK population in general.

The sample

The sample consisted of 50 young people, 24 of whom were male and 36 of whom described their ethnic origin as 'white'. Half the sample were living with their parents, 9 were living in temporary hostels or on the street and the remainder were renting their current accommodation. Just over half the sample (27) were currently in some form of education, 13 had full-time work and the remaining 10 were unemployed.

All participants reported that they had consumed alcohol at some point in their lives. The majority (94%) also reported that they had used cannabis at least once in their life. In addition, the most commonly used illicit drugs were amphetamines (70%), ecstasy (54%) and LSD (42%).

Drug and alcohol use played a major role in the leisure activities chosen by this sample of young people. For most, the only time when they used drugs or alcohol was when they were with their friends: when alone they filled their time with other activities. For some, socialising with friends was virtually synonymous with substance use of one form or another.

In general, substance use tended to be associated with positive aspects of the young people's lives and was seen as enhancing many social activities. However, for those respondents who reported regular use of opiates and benzodiazepines, their drug use was more likely to be described as a means of coping with negative experiences (events or mood states). The use of opiates and benzodiazepines was also more common amongst those respondents who were experiencing social problems, such as home-lessness.

Influences on drug and alcohol-related decisions

The study examined both 'individual factors' and 'social/contextual factors' which underpin decisions about substance use. At the individual level, six separate factors were identified: functions for drug use, expectancies, current state, gender, commitments and boundaries. At the social/contextual level, five factors were identified: environment, availability, finances, social influences and media influences.

Individual influences

Functions

A major influence on drug and alcohol-related decisions at an individual level was the specific 'function'* that the individual wanted their substance use to fulfil. The functions for use included facilitating activity (such as work or dancing for long periods), changing mood or helping to manage the effects from other drugs.

Different drugs served different functions for the consumer, although some were substituted for others on certain occasions.

Expectancies

The second major influence identified in this study was the individual's expectancies about the effects of a given substance. These drug-related expectancies seemed to become more sophisticated as the user gathered experience and learned to take additional factors into account, such as dosage consumed or other concurrent substance use.

* The function of the use of a drug can be defined as the benefit the user perceives from consuming it.

Current state

Some respondents described how their current psychological or physical state impacted on their expectancies concerning the effects of a substance. For example, feeling depressed or tired might affect the drug and alcohol-related decisions that they made.

Gender influences

There were several accounts of differences in the *types* of substances that males and females preferred: younger respondents (16- and 17-year-olds) suggested that females drank more alcohol than the males who preferred to smoke cannabis instead. In contrast, females amongst the older respondents were reported to prefer the physical effects from such stimulants as amphetamines, whilst the males enjoyed the perceptual distortions from hallucinogens.

Commitments

Commitments were often considered by respondents when making drug or alcohol-related decisions. These might influence an individual to use less of a substance or to choose an alternative drug type from which they expected to experience less negative after-effects.

Boundaries

Respondents with similar drug-related experiences tended to share the same basic boundaries in determining what they would or would not use. Using heroin, crack and injecting any drug was perceived by most as more dangerous than other forms of drug use. For some, cocaine powder was grouped alongside heroin and crack, whereas other, more experienced drug users, regarded cocaine as similar to ecstasy and amphetamines.

Social/contextual influences

Environment

It was common for respondents to talk about needing to be in the 'right sort of place' when using certain substances, particularly those with hallucinogenic effects. The 'wrong' sort of environment could precipitate the decision to abstain.

Availability

Substitution was commonly reported on occasions when a drug of preference was unavailable. For example, amphetamines were sometimes used in place of ecstasy.

There were also reports that lack of availability had prompted the initiation into the use of other drug types. One example of this was initiating into the use of LSD on an occasion when cannabis was unavailable.

Finances

The estimated amount of disposable income for the sample ranged from £14 to £420 per week.

The average amount spent on clothes and shoes was very similar to that spent on alcohol and other drugs. For most respondents the total spent per month on cigarettes, alcohol and other drugs combined was at least half of their monthly disposable income.

Several cannabis smokers reported that, on occasions, they would sell small quantities of this drug to friends in order to pay for their own supply. However, there was little evidence of similar small-scale selling of other drug types.

Social influences

Some respondents differentiated between different circles of friends according to the group's drug or alcohol use preferences. These young people reported that they tended to tailor their substance use to fit in with the norms of the particular group with which they were socialising.

The concept of 'peer pressure' was familiar to the respondents and was often mentioned without prompting. However, there was a general consensus that substance use was engaged in through choice rather than as a result of pressure.

There was some evidence suggesting that close friends or 'best friends' played a particularly important role at the initiation into use of a substance by providing additional support to an individual. Friends were also reported to influence both reductions and escalations in substance use.

Media influences

National news stories of ecstasy-related deaths were cited by some interviewees as having contributed to their decision to abstain from using this drug. Other respondents had either dismissed the accounts completely or offered explanations for the deaths which cast the victims as incompetent drug users. In contrast, the lack of high profile media stories relating to amphetamines seemed to have led many to deduce that this was far less dangerous than ecstasy, and so they were motivated to use this drug instead.

Transitions

Changes in substance use patterns (both escalations and reductions) seemed to be influenced by similar factors to those identified as influential over decisions to use drugs in general (i.e. function, expectancies, commitments, etc.).

Limiting drug use

Many respondents had established methods for limiting their substance use. Strategies described fell into two categories: limiting use by dose (amount) in order to avoid ill effects or continuing to use until time or money dictated that they should stop. Using time or money to limit use was a deliberate strategy for some, although for others this was by default rather than through conscious decision.

The data also suggest that an individual who used 'dose limiting' strategies for one drug might use a different strategy to limit use of another.

INTRODUCTION

Becoming an adult in contemporary society involves a transition to independence. A young person takes increasing responsibility for making key decisions regarding their lifestyle and behaviour. This process of development lays down important preferences concerning how an individual sees themselves (i.e. their identity) and their role in society. An array of ongoing decisions are made concerning preferences for music, dress and other aspects of lifestyle. One such area of decision-making concerns drug and alcohol use. At some point, virtually all young people must decide whether or not to use psychoactive substances and, if they decide to do so, to what extent. While these decisions may engage little more than a few seconds of conscious attention, it is nevertheless vital to explore these processes in order to increase our understanding of why so many young people choose to use drugs and alcohol.

1.1 Background

In the UK, recent population surveys have reported that approximately 50% of young people sampled between the ages of 16 and 24 years have tried an illicit drug on at least one occasion (Ramsay and Spiller 1997; Health Education Authority 1997). The 1996 British Crime Survey found that approximately 35% of 16–19-year-olds had used cannabis, as had 42% of those between 20 and 24 (Ramsay and Spiller 1997). The next most commonly used drug was amphetamines (16% of the younger group having tried this and 21% of the older group), followed by LSD (10% and 14% respectively) and then ecstasy (9% and 13%). In contrast, figures for cocaine use are around 2% for 16–19-year-olds and 6% for 20–24-year-olds. Use of heroin is reported by 1% or less of both the above age groups. However, for many young people, their substance use is only ever experimental and never becomes habitual or problematic.

Recent research has provided evidence that the number of young people reporting that they have been in situations where drugs have been offered to them is also increasing (Balding 1996; HEA 1997; Aldridge et al. 1995). This suggests that a significant number of young people have been offered drugs, but for various reasons have declined them (Fountain et al., in press). With the increasing prevalence of exposure to substance use, it is possible that the decision to use is made quite lightly by some, perhaps with little consideration of the positive or negative effects of this action. Nevertheless, if a behaviour is actioned on some occasions and not others, it would suggest that some sort of appraisal and decision-making process takes place. However, remarkably little is known about the primary motivating factors which influence the decision to use or decline a substance when the opportunity arises. This project was designed to examine these issues and to highlight the specific factors that young people cite as influencing their drug and alcohol-related decisions. A more detailed understanding of these processes could play a vital role in the design, implementation and evaluation of drug education and prevention programmes.

To date, studies of how young people make decisions have placed particular emphasis on the relative influence of their parents and peers. Several studies have found that parents are particularly influential when a young person is making long-term decisions about their future, whereas the opinions of peers are perceived as more important when resolving dilemmas concerning dress, social events, alcohol use or other aspects of an individual's current lifestyle (Brittain 1963; Sebald and White 1980; Wilks 1986). These findings indicate that decisions about substance use are likely to be influenced mainly by the peer group, as part of their shared experience of life and leisure activities. Indeed, the available literature on this issue seems to point clearly to a direct link between peers and substance use; the substance use of peers has been found to be the largest single predictor of an individual's use (Swadi 1992; Nurco, Balter & Kinlock 1994; Fergusson, Horwood & Lynskey 1995). However there is little consensus as to how this finding should be interpreted. Much of the literature in this area has viewed the concept of 'peer pressure' as a mediating influence on an individual's substance use. This concept underlies several resistance skills-based drug prevention programmes. One example is project DARE (Drug Abuse Resistance Education), which has been implemented extensively in the USA and more recently in the UK. Unfortunately, despite the widespread delivery of DARE-based initiatives, there is little published evidence for their effectiveness (Rosenbaum et al. 1994; Ennet et al. 1994: Hurry & Lloyd 1997). The orientation of DARE and other similar programmes regards young people as rather passive recipients of external influences, rather than independent individuals who make active appraisals of their behaviour. In this way the DARE perspective could be described as inherently conservative, and it is possible that it has been embraced so widely because of its perception of young people as essentially passive and malleable to both positive and negative external influences. This perhaps provides a convenient, unthreatening explanation for parents or teachers as to why adolescents deviate from what society might perceive as preferred patterns of behaviour.

Recent explanations for the association between peers and substance use have adopted a more dynamic view of the individual's role. For example, Coggans and McKellar (1994) argue that the association between peers and substance use should not be interpreted as 'peer pressure' but as 'peer preference' – the favouring or choosing of some friends and associates over others. Unlike 'peer pressure', this term grants the individual an active role in their choice of peer networks. Fountain, Boys and Griffiths (1997) use the term 'peer influence' and argue that it is more neutral than both 'pressure' and 'preference', and is therefore appropriate for both positive and negative circumstances.

Oetting and Beauvais (1987) highlight the importance of clarifying the exact meaning of 'peer' or 'peer group' in their 'peer cluster theory'. They argue that any young person is likely to be associated with, or part of, several distinct social groupings, all of which could be referred to as a 'peer group'. They suggest that it is important to differentiate between these general groupings and smaller, more defined groups which could be labelled as 'peer clusters'. It is these small, primary influencing groups that are seen as the most dominant influences in adolescent substance use. Other secondary influences include environmental factors (such as poverty, family or the community) and individual factors (such as personality traits, values or beliefs).

Whatever the relative weighting of these influences, research suggests that the behavioural patterns which many young people exhibit, and which define their life-styles, are very similar to those of their friends. These include smoking, drinking and drug use as well as sexual behaviour (Billy, Rodgers & Udry 1984; Kandel 1978b; Tolson & Urberg 1993). Three main reasons have been suggested for these similarities. Firstly, that socio-economic conditions help bring similar types of young people together, thus providing the opportunity for friendships to develop. Secondly, that young people may gravitate towards individuals who are similar to them, selecting them to be their friends; or, thirdly, through spending time together and engaging in mutual activities, friends become more similar through the process of 'mutual socialisation'. Kandel (1978a) examined the changes in substance-related behaviours over a one-year period among groups of friends and suggested that similarities between friends were accounted for by both selection and socialisation in approximately equal proportions. However, these processes are not necessarily concurrent. In another study of young people, Fisher and Baumann (1988) examined smoking and drinking patterns and concluded that selection was the more important process.

An alternative approach, influenced by psychological theories of health behaviour, has been to examine the connections between individual and social/contextual motivations for substance use. Instead of viewing young people as passive victims of their social and environmental circumstances, they are seen as rational and active decision-makers who consider the costs and benefits of substance use (e.g. Langer & Warheit 1992; Ajzen 1985, 1988). Several researchers from this perspective have explored the range of reasons and motivations reported for using a substance. Some reasons have been quite broad (e.g. to feel better) or have related to the specific role or *function* for use (e.g. to increase self-confidence). A limitation of much of this literature has been the discussion of all illicit substances together or the distinction between cannabis and 'hard drugs' only (Newcomb et al. 1988; McKay et al. 1992; Kamali & Steer 1976; Carman 1979; Butler, Gunderson & Bruni 1981; Cato 1992). Consequently, findings have provided little practical information to guide education programmes. In contrast, Johnston and O'Malley (1986) differentiated reasons for the use of alcohol, cannabis, LSD, amphetamines, barbiturates, tranquillisers, cocaine, heroin and other opiates in a sample of young people. However, these studies have all employed quantitative techniques, which only allow respondents to report predetermined reasons for their chosen substance use. The qualitative design of this study allowed a much closer, more detailed examination of these issues and how motivations might interact with other influences on drug and alcohol-related decision-making.

An important mediating influence in substance-related decisions is what effects a person expects when they use it. However, these 'expectancies' are not necessarily based solely on the pharmacological effects of a substance, but may be influenced by reports from peers and cultural learning (Stacy, Leigh & Weingardt 1994). Jaffe and Kilbey (1994) found that different groups of adult cocaine users (categorised as 'abusers', 'experimenters' and 'non-users') had quite different expectancies concerning the effects of this drug and that these were powerful predictors of use. Research has also explored alcohol expectancies amongst young people. One such study, for example, found that alcohol expectancies predicted the future likelihood of drink-related problems in young people (Christiansen *et al.* 1989). These findings have led researchers to suggest that trying to modify the expectancies held by individuals in relation to alcohol or cocaine use, or teaching alternative (drug-free) ways to obtain these expected outcomes, could make an important contribution to therapeutic interventions (Jaffe & Kilbey 1994; Goldman, Brown & Christiansen 1987). The impact of expectancies on decision-making concerning the use of other drugs has received little attention. Nevertheless, it seems likely that expectancies can play a major role in mediating decisions concerning the use of other substances.

1.2 Types of decisions and related influences

Decisions about substance use do not cease once a young person has initiated the use of a drug. Instead, the individual is faced with such decisions as whether to use the substance on subsequent occasions and, if so, how much of it to consume. In a study of drug use amongst adolescents, Glasner and Loughlin (1987) observed that nearly all of their subjects, including the heaviest users, decided against using drugs on certain occasions. They suggested that all participants in their study had fairly rigid rules governing their drug-using behaviour and had certain boundaries that they would not cross. The majority of their sample regarded their drug use as a result of self-controlled choices.

In a discussion of how young people make decisions about drug and alcohol use, it is important to acknowledge that there are different types of drug-related decisions to be made, such as

- whether to experiment with illicit drugs;
- which of a range of available substances to use;
- when to use drugs or alcohol and when not to;
- how much to use on an occasion and when to stop.

Whilst the factors that influence these different decisions may be similar, the relative importance of these components could vary. This report focuses primarily on the influences which mediate decisions concerning the first three types. However, there are also sections which address the fourth, in addition to factors which influence increases or decreases in use of a substance (see Chapters 7 and 8).

1.3 Framework for the present study

A review of the relevant literature and informal discussions with young people suggested that a range of factors underlie drug and alcohol-related decision-making. Table 1.1 summarises the main factors identified for the purposes of this study:

Table 1.1 Decision-making influences

Individual influences	Social/contextual influences
Functions for substance use	Environment
Physical/ psychological state	Availability
Expectancies	Drug prices
Gender	Family influences
Commitments	Peer influences
Boundaries	Social communication/media

The framework established to guide the present study perceives influences on decision-making as operating from both specific and general levels. We regard the purpose that substance use plays for a young person to be central to decision-making amongst this population. We have described this as the specific 'function' that the user is seeking to fulfil through their substance use. An example of this might be the use of drugs in order to relieve boredom. This factor could interact with the expectancies that the individual has for substance use: for example, if someone is looking for a substance to help them to keep awake, and they believe that cannabis will make them drowsy, then they are likely to decide against using this particular substance on this occasion. The current psychological or physical state of an individual might also affect the expectancies concerning a particular substance (such as, 'If I'm feeling "down" then alcohol makes me more depressed') and thus impact on the decision-making process too. Our approach stands in sharp contrast to previous etiological theories, which have emphasised predispositional vulnerabilities and peer pressure.

It is also worth noting that different people might have different ideas of what sorts of behaviour are acceptable and what are not. In other words their behavioural boundaries differ. For example, some might regard using cocaine in a powder form as acceptable, but disapprove of smoking crack cocaine. This could affect the decisions concerning their choice of behaviour.

At the general level, various factors might influence the context in which substance use could take place. For example, an individual might feel that the environment they are in (such as a crowded nightclub) is not appropriate for using a particular substance (such as LSD). Other factors influencing decisions might include financial considerations and ease of supply: if a drug is not readily available, the considerable effort to obtain it might not seem worthwhile. Finally, such factors as family and peer influences (discussed earlier in this chapter), could also be classified at the general level.

Our discussion of these issues is structured in such a way that each of the above factors are examined in turn. Before these issues are addressed, the first chapters examine the methods employed in the research process and the characteristics of the sample. These are followed by an account of how the respondents filled their spare time and the role that drug and alcohol use played within their repertoires of leisure activities.

2 PURPOSE AND OBJECTIVES OF THE STUDY

The main purpose of this study was to explore the key factors which influence the decisions made about drug and alcohol use amongst young people. The study employed a qualitative design to meet the following objectives:

- To describe the primary factors which influence the decisions that young people make about drug and alcohol use.
- To assess the role played by peer networks in influencing drug and alcohol use by young people.
- To examine the range of functions that drug and alcohol use serves for young people and how substance use fits into their repertoires of leisure activities and consumable items.

The study was designed to explore these areas in detail and to allow additional relevant themes to emerge. The majority of the report addresses the interplay between different factors which mediate the drug and alcohol-related decisions made by young people. Material is also presented on the influences cited by participants as having particular impact on transitions from experimental to regular substance use, together with factors affecting decisions concerning how much of a substance is consumed on a using occasion. The report concludes with a synthesis of the key findings, followed by recommendations for further research into this area.

3 METHODOLOGY

Much of the existing body of research on young people and substance use has used quantitative data collection techniques, relying mainly on self-completion questionnaires. The common practice has been to recruit samples through educational establishments, rather than through more informal channels. This approach is economical and enables a rapid sample recruitment together with the collection of large data sets. However, these advantages could be at the expense of both the reliability and depth of information collected. This study used a qualitative face-to-face interview, complemented by a short interviewer-administered quantitative questionnaire, to investigate the factors that influence drug and alcohol-related decision-making. As far as possible in the available time, participants were recruited from informal settings. Those who were recruited through a college or another educational establishment were reassured that neither teaching staff nor parents would have access to their responses. All participants were informed that the data collected was both anonymous and confidential and that participation was voluntary. This helped to ensure that the accuracy and detail of the data were maximised.

3.1 Recruitment of the sample

All participants were recruited from the South of England, though some were from other parts of the UK and had recently moved in order to study or to seek employment. All but three of the participants in the study had tried an illicit drug. The sample size was chosen on the basis of being practically achievable within the time and resources available and was sufficiently large to allow meaningful exploration of the key interests. Respondents were recruited using snowballing techniques from seven starting points, with the aim of obtaining a range of ages, occupations (and thus incomes) and social backgrounds (see Boys *et al.* in press a for more detail). This recruitment technique is recognised to be an effective way of generating samples from hidden populations where no formal sampling frame is available (Van Meter 1990).

3.2 The interview schedule

The initial interview schedule was semi-structured and covered a wide range of topics. As the study progressed and key themes were identified, the interviews became more focused. Respondents were encouraged to give as much information as they wanted to in response to questions, and answers were further probed by the interviewer. Prompt cards bearing the names of various drug types were used in order to facilitate discussion. The main topic areas included in the interviews were the following:

• The influence of peers on drug-related decisions.

- The influence that the substance-related behaviours of close friends had on respondents' decisions.
- The types of boundaries set by peer groups and how these influence decisions at the individual level.
- The beliefs and expectancies about the effects of different drugs (on behaviour, moods and emotions) and how these factors impact on drug-related decisions.
- Perceptions of the different functions served by substance use.
- How drug and alcohol use fits into the wider repertoires of leisure activities and consumable items that young people purchase or obtain.
- Gender differences in substance use patterns.

Interviews were tape-recorded with the interviewee's consent and subsequently transcribed. This method was chosen to create an informal atmosphere in which fuller responses were more likely to be given than if data were written down in front of the respondent. There was no evidence that this method compromised the quality or quantity of the data collected: participants seemed happy to be recorded and quickly appeared to forget about the presence of the tape recorder.* Respondents received expenses for travel and to compensate them for the time they spent being interviewed.

3.3 Core quantitative data

Each participant in the study also completed a short, structured, researcher-administered questionnaire at the start of the interview. This was designed to complement the in-depth interviews by collecting basic demographic details quickly and efficiently. Lifetime use of 11 substances and the consumption patterns of 5 target substances (alcohol, cannabis, amphetamines, ecstasy and LSD) selected for discussion, were recorded based on procedures developed by Marsden *et al.* (1998). These methods were selected as they have been shown to be both valid and reliable in the rapid assessment of the frequency and typical intensity of substance use from adults' self-reports.

Data were collected between July and October 1997. Interviews were conducted in a range of community locations; the majority in respondents' homes or those of friends. Each interview took an average of one hour to complete.

3.4 Validity and interpretation of the data

The interview schedule was devised to cross-check answers from the questionnaire and therefore highlight any inconsistencies in self-reported substance use. Prompt questions

* Presentation of verbatim quotes in this report: A decision was taken to remove a small number of expletives from some verbatim quotes presented in this report. These are indicated by [[ ]]. For ease of reading, alternative words have been used in some of these instances.

were used which were highly face-valid. However, accounts of events could not be verified in this manner.

A substantial body of evidence exists for the validity of self-reported data on drug use from adult clinical samples where reports have been favourably compared with objective measures, such as hair analysis or urinalysis (e.g. Magura *et al.* 1987, 1992). The literature on self-report for younger, recreational users is smaller. However, after detailed discussion of the available evidence, Oetting and Beauvais (1990) concluded that self-reports of drug use by adolescents are generally truthful and reliable.

It should be noted that research which relies on self-report hinges on the assumption that respondents not only accurately report what they believe to have occurred ('veridicality': Bonito, Nurco & Shaffer 1976; Nurco 1985), but have an accurate know-ledge or understanding of occurrences to report on. However, given that a principal aim of qualitative research is to 'access the phenomena of interest from the perspective of the subject; to describe what is going on; and to emphasise the importance of both context and process' (Buston *et al.* 1998, p. 198), an accurate report of what the individual believes to have occurred is of greater importance than the actual sequence of events.

We do not suggest that the behaviour, experiences or opinions described in this report are representative of all young people. The sample was chosen to comprise individuals whose experience of substance use was in excess of national norms for this age range so that the key areas could be discussed in depth. However, the data highlight potentially crucial issues that warrant further in-depth investigation, employing quantitative techniques with a larger, randomised sample of young people (see Chapter 9, 'Summary and recommendations' for more details).

3.5 Data analysis

A synthesis of analytic induction and grounded theory (Glaser & Strauss 1967) was used to guide the analysis of the qualitative data. Essentially, this meant that analysis was not carried out as a distinct and separate stage, but interacted with the planning and execution of the fieldwork. A progressive focusing technique was employed whereby initial interviews identified the issues which were significant to individuals from the drug-using networks under study. Both the research process and findings were grounded in the data rather than in a pre-set itinerary and were guided by issues that seemed significant to the informants in addition to the concerns of the research agenda. Key themes that emerged from the data were categorised for further inter-viewing and analytical purposes. These ultimately formed the main structure of the report. Every major theme (a total of 30) received a code number, and the data from the transcriptions were filed under these. Within each theme, transcripts were further coded to indicate the substance type being discussed. Thus extracts from each hour-long interview could be coded into single or multiple categories and could be as long as several paragraphs or as short as a phrase.

A legitimate criticism of some studies using qualitative methods is that they support conclusions with highly selective quotations from informants (e.g. Davies & Best 1996). We sought to guard against this: the grounded theory approach meant that interpretations were fed back into the data-gathering techniques and thus directed the collection of further data. When all the data pertaining to a category were collated, it was possible to establish whether or not comments were universally or specifically employed by the sample. 'Inconvenient' deviations from the norm were not disregarded.

THE SAMPLE CHARACTERISTICS

4.1 Personal and social demographics

The sample comprised 50 young people, 24 of whom were male. The mean age of the group was 18.5 years (median = 18 years) and all were between 16 and 21 years old. The majority of the sample (36) described themselves as 'white'. Nine gave their ethnic origin as African-Caribbean or Black British; 3 as mixed race and 2 as Asian. Half the sample were living with their parents. Fifteen lived in privately rented accommodation, 9 in rented council or housing association homes and a further 9 were in temporary hostel accommodation or homeless.

Just over half of the sample (27) were in some sort of education at the time of the interview. Thirteen respondents (9 males) had full-time employment and all but one of these individuals worked in an 'unskilled' job. The remaining 10 were unemployed at the time of the interview, most of these (7) were male.

The amount of disposable income* that respondents had ranged from £14 per week (a 16-year-old female, living with her parents) to £420 per week (a homeless 17-year-old male, making money from begging and petty crime). The average amount was £75 per week.

4.2 Substance use experience

This report primarily focuses on the substances most commonly used by the sample: alcohol, cannabis and the three 'dance drugs' (amphetamines, ecstasy and LSD). Use of other drugs is addressed at points where this appeared to be of particular significance to the overall discussion.

Everyone interviewed had tried alcohol and all but two respondents (one male and one female) reported that they had smoked a cigarette. Reflecting recent UK population prevalence studies, the most commonly used illicit drug was cannabis: the majority of the sample (47) reporting that they had tried this drug on at least one occasion. The next most commonly used substances were the so-called 'dance drugs' (amphetamines, ecstasy and then LSD). Ten people had tried heroin and four (two male and two female) had injected a drug at some point in their lives. These rates of substance use appear high, given the prevalence data quoted in the introduction to this report. However, it should be noted that this was not a randomised sample selected for prevalence estimation purposes, and participants were to some extent self-selecting. It is therefore

* 'Disposable income' was defined as money in excess of that which was needed to pay for accommodation and bills.

possible that those with an interest in substance use stemming from their own experimentation, were more likely to participate.

Respondents were asked how old they were when they first used each of 11 substances. Over half of the sample had used cigarettes, alcohol and cannabis by the age of 14. This contrasts with the average age of first use for the three 'dance drugs', which was 16 or over (see Table 4.1).

Table 4.1 Substance use history (*n* = 50)

Substance	Male (*n* = 24)	Female (*n* = 26)	Total	Av. age of first use (range)	
Cigarettes	23	25	48	13.2	(7–18)
Alcohol	23	26	49	13.6	(11–18)
Cannabis	23	24	47	14.5	(10–18)
Amphetamines	18	17	35	16.0	(13–19)
Ecstasy	15	12	27	16.8	(13–19)
LSD	13	8	21	16.3	(12–20)
Cocaine powder	9	7	16	–	–
Heroin	8	2	10	–	–
Benzodiazepines	4	2	6	–	–
Other opiates	4	1	5	–	–
Crack cocaine	2	0	2	–	–

Table 4.2 Total number of occasions of use (lifetime) for each substance

Drug type	Number	Once only	2–10	11–20	21–100	100+
		%	%	%	%	%
Cigarettes	48	2	10	2	4	81
Alcohol	49	0	2	8	10	80
Cannabis	47	4	4	6	21	64
Amphetamines	35	6	23	17	43	11
Ecstasy	27	15	26	11	22	26
LSD	21	19	29	14	29	9
Heroin	10*	44	22	0	0	22

* Data was unavailable for one case

As a measure of experience, respondents were asked to estimate the total number of occasions on which they had used each substance. This was facilitated by the use of a prompt card showing frequency categories. Most respondents who had used alcohol and cannabis had done so on over 100 occasions. Such frequency of use was less common for the 'dance drugs', though 19 of those who had ever used amphetamines had done so on at least 21 different occasions, with four reporting use exceeding 100 times. Slightly fewer of those who had tried ecstasy (13) reported over 20 occasions of use. For LSD, limited use was much more common, with 10 young people reporting 10 occasions of use or less. Nearly half of those who had tried heroin had done so on only one occasion (see Table 4.2).

Recent use of different substances

Defining what constitutes a 'current user' varies according to the substance being discussed. For example, whilst using several times a week may be common for some substances (such as cigarettes, alcohol or cannabis), such frequent use of the stimulants or hallucinogens might not be expected. Consequently, rather than attempting to define 'current use' or 'regular use', measures of the frequency and intensity of recent use were taken.

More than 80% of the respondents who had used alcohol and cannabis had done so within the three months prior to the interview. These figures contrast with those for the three 'dance drugs', which are much lower, though if use within the last year is considered, the differences for ecstasy and amphetamines are smaller. However, of those who had tried LSD, recent use of this drug was much less common than for the other substances, with 48% of those who had used this drug having used it within the year prior to interview (see Table 4.3).

Table 4.3 Profile of recent substance use (*n* = 50)

Drug Type	Number	Last year %	Last 3 months %
Cigarettes	48	85	85
Alcohol	50	100	92
Cannabis	47	89	83
Amphetamines	35	77	60
Ecstasy	27	85	63
LSD	21	48	38
Heroin	10	50	30

Frequency and intensity of substance use

Recent frequency of use was measured using estimations of the number of days of use in the last three months. The responses were then combined into four frequency categories ranging from '6–7 days a week', to 'less than monthly'. After cigarettes, cannabis was the substance most frequently used on a very regular (i.e. daily) basis. Thirty-nine per cent of those who had used cannabis in the last 90 days reported using on six or seven days a week. This compares with 18% of those who had used alcohol in the last three months. However, over three-quarters (34) were drinking at least once a week at the time of the interview. Only two people reported that they had drunk alcohol less than once a month in the past three months and four had abstained completely. In contrast to use of cigarettes, alcohol and cannabis, use of amphetamines, ecstasy and LSD tended to be less than once a week (see Table 4.4).

Table 4.4 Frequency of use in the last three months

Use in last 3 months	Cigarettes n = 40 %	Alcohol n = 44 %	Cannabis n = 38 %	Amphetamines n = 20 %	Ecstasy n = 17 %	LSD n = 8 %
6 or 7 days a week	85	18	39	5	0	0
1–5 days a week	8	59	47	30	35	37
1–3 times a month	5	14	8	30	53	25
Less than monthly	2	9	5	35	12	37

The quantity or 'intensity' of substance use was measured as the amount used on a typical using day during the last three months. Common dose units (such as 'cannabis joints' or 'ecstasy tablets') were used to record this information. However, these results must obviously be interpreted with care as drug concentrations and dose units may vary.

The results indicate a wide range of 'typical doses' for all substance types amongst this sample. For example, a typical drinking day for some people meant that they consumed only one unit, yet for others the typical amount consumed was much larger. On average the amount reported was 9.5 units. Similarly, for cannabis the amount consumed on an average day ranged from 1 to 25 'joints' with a mean of 5.1; amphetamines ranged from a third of a gram to 2.5 grams (mean = 1.3 g); ecstasy ranged from half a tablet to 6 tablets (mean = 1.75); and LSD ranged from 1 to 3 tablets with a mean of 1 (see Table 4.5). Given that the 1995 *Sensible drinking* report by the Department of Health suggests that consistently drinking more than 4 units (for males) or 3 units (for females) in a day is inadvisable for adults, it seems that the majority of young people in this study were regularly consuming more than twice the recommended limits. There are no figures for illicit drug use with which to compare the other amounts used.

Table 4.5 Amount used on a 'typical using day' in past three months

Substance	Number of people	Range	Mean
Number of cigarettes	40	1–30	13.0
Units of alcohol	44	1–26	9.5
Number of cannabis joints	38	1–25	5.1
Amphetamines (g)	20	0.3–2.5	1.3
Number of ecstasy tablets	17	0.5–6.0	1.75
Number of LSD tablets	8	1–3	1.0

5 LEISURE TIME

Some drug prevention initiatives have presumed that young people use drugs and alcohol because they are bored and have nothing else with which to fill their leisure time. This has contributed to the development of some preventative programmes which use a diversionary activity approach. Whilst it would be wrong to dismiss this idea completely, as it clearly can contribute to an explanation for substance use, the issue is without doubt more complex. This chapter explores the types of leisure activities engaged in by respondents and examines the role of drug and alcohol use within this repertoire.

Over 70% of the sample reported going to a pub, bar or nightclub several times each month. Meeting with friends was also endorsed as a regular leisure activity by most respondents, and many of the younger respondents, reported 'hanging around' on the street or in a park.

When asked how they filled their spare time, the list of activities cited by respondents included:

- meeting up at friends' houses,
- going to the pub,
- going to nightclubs,
- watching television/videos,
- shopping,
- playing computer games,
- going to the cinema,
- listening to music,
- practising DJ-ing,
- participating in a sport,
- 'hanging around' in the park/ on the street,
- attending a youth club.

Perhaps the most significant finding was that virtually all respondents mentioned some form of activity which involved substance use when asked what they did when they met up with friends, (for example, going to the pub, meeting up at friends' houses and smoking cannabis/drinking alcohol or going to nightclubs). The data show that drug and alcohol use play a major role in the leisure activities chosen by this group of young people. Indeed, not only were substance-related activities very common, but a large proportion of the sample reported that they almost always used alcohol, cannabis or one of the dance drugs when they met up with their friends. In other words, for some, socialising with friends was virtually synonymous with some form of substance use, as the following extracts illustrate:

Q. Do you spend time with your friends without using drugs or alcohol?

> A. When we're together we normally get wrecked [intoxicated], unless we've got college work to do, then we sometimes get together to do work. (MALE aged 20)

Q. Do you spend time with your friends without using drugs or alcohol?

> A. Yeah . . . but not very often, we normally drink. We might go round the shops or to the cinema . . . I think it's 'cos of a lack of things to do that we normally go out and get drunk. It just becomes a way of life to meet in the pub and get drunk. (FEMALE aged 19)

For many, socialising was the only time when drug or alcohol use took place. When alone or with family, use was uncommon. However, of the few respondents who did report substance use when alone, the drug most commonly used was cannabis, and, even less frequently, alcohol or amphetamines. Use of other drugs outside of social settings (such as LSD or ecstasy) were virtually never reported.

Special occasions

Alcohol use is often associated with special occasions, for example, toasting people on their birthdays or if they have achieved something significant. It is common amongst adults to celebrate an occasion by spending more money than usual on food or alcohol. In a similar way the young people interviewed for this study tended to associate special occasions with an increased consumption of alcohol or another drug of choice.

Q. How would a special event or occasion be different from other evenings?

> A. We'd probably drink more or probably do more drugs ... (FEMALE aged 18)

A few respondents also suggested that different, perhaps more expensive drug types (such as cocaine), might be chosen to mark a special occasion.

Q. If there's a special event or occasion, what sort of things might you and your friends do together to celebrate?

> A. Probably go out clubbing. We'd arrange to go somewhere different and arrange for more people to go.

Q. Would you use different drugs on a special occasion?

> A. Depends. We might get some coke, rather than doing pills [ecstasy]. (FEMALE aged 20)

Q. So how do you decide when to take cocaine and when not to have it?

> A. Well, I haven't had it for ages . . . if it's for a special occasion then I'll get it in, but a while back I did do a bit too much. I try to cut all my Es [ecstasy tablets] and stuff just down to special occasions, but it doesn't always work! (FEMALE aged 18)

For some, a special occasion was cited as a motive to use drugs in a context where they might usually use alcohol. One 20-year-old male explained why he felt the use of illicit drugs on a special occasion was preferable to alcohol. He found that it was a means of ensuring that the group definitely had 'a good night out', as he thought that the dose needed for an optimum effect from ecstasy was easier to gauge than that needed for alcohol:

A. It's not like you have to use things [drugs] but you know that makes things better . . . if we were going out for someone's birthday, if we were going clubbing, we would use pills [ecstasy] and stuff because then you don't have to worry about whether or not it's going to be a good night … 'cos it always is.

Q. Whereas if you're just drinking . . . ?

A. Yeah, well, if you're drinking, it's just trying to time the amount of drink that you have 'cos you can not have enough drink (and so you're still a bit straight) . . . and if you have too much then you're too pissed to do anything! (MALE aged 20)

MAIN FINDINGS: FACTORS RELATED TO DECISION-MAKING

6.1 The functions of drug and alcohol use

An important hypothesis advanced in this study is that the perceived functions for drug and alcohol use influence decisions about consumption. We define the 'function' of substance use as the benefit that an individual perceives from using it. For example, a young person might choose to drink alcohol in a social situation to help them to relax and to feel more confident, or they might use strong coffee or caffeine pills to help them to stay awake. It may be regarded as axiomatic that psychoactive substances are used because of their effects. However, these effects can only be understood in the context of an individual's psychological state, expectations about the social context of use and of other substance use of similar and contrasting actions. In general, these functions may be expected to fall within the broad dimensions of sedation, stimulation, disphoria and perceptual alteration, as to some extent they depend on the pharmacological effects of the substance. Thus the likelihood of deciding to use a drug with sedative effects is increased if a person wants help in getting to sleep and a stimulant, such as caffeine or amphetamines, might be chosen if they want to feel more energetic or wakeful. However, as the effects from a drug will differ at different dose concentrations, in different settings or when used in combination with other drugs, so might the corresponding functions for using under these circumstances.

One of the aims for the present study was to explore the range of functions that substance use fulfilled for the sample. Given the qualitative nature of the study, questions were not asked directly about why drugs were used or what functions use fulfilled for the participants. Instead respondents were asked to describe the circumstances under which they tended to use different drugs. The discussion was then developed from this starting point with a view to obtaining as much detailed information as possible.

In general, the participants in this study were very articulate about the reasons and functions for their substance use. In this chapter we explore the range of different functions commonly described for each substance, drawing evidence from the in-depth interviews. The discussion focuses on six substance types: cannabis, amphetamines, ecstasy, LSD, opiates and alcohol. The section concludes with an exploration of the complex issues of poly-substance use and concurrent use. The functions that using different drugs at the same time might fulfil for the user are also discussed.

Cannabis

Almost all the respondents in this study (94%) had tried cannabis. Nearly two-thirds of these had used it on more than 100 occasions and a further 21% had used it more than 20 times. Perhaps reflecting its status as the most widely used illicit drug amongst this sample, the functions for cannabis use were reported to be diverse. The most popular purpose for smoking this drug was to relieve stress or to aid relaxation, as two of the male respondents explained:

> The way society is today [everyone] gets stressed at something, you know, and so [smoking cannabis is] just a way to . . . I mean, I get stressed very easily and I don't like it because it upsets me and it upsets other people and it makes me ill . . . so I guess it's a way of keeping healthy. (MALE aged 21)

> A. . . . there were other things – family stress – not getting on with my Dad.

Q. So how did smoking [cannabis] help?

> A. Shut it out and gave me my own thing, and the people I met through it were all very nice people and I made a few really good friends. We used to just sit and smoke all the time. (MALE aged 21)

Others reported that they liked using cannabis because it helped them to feel more relaxed and less inhibited in social situations. Another 21-year-old, with considerable illicit drug use experience, explained how he saw the function of cannabis smoking in social situations as similar to that of using alcohol:

> The more you're stoned, the more relaxed you feel . . . I think it's more of a social kind of drug. If everyone's nicely stoned then you're not pressured to talk if you don't want to. You can always sit there and listen. I find when I'm straight . . . I can sit in a room with somebody and if I've got nothing to say then I'd feel uncomfortable . . . but if I was stoned or slightly drunk, that uncomfortable silence wouldn't be an uncomfortable silence anymore. You wouldn't feel pressured to say anything if you didn't want to. (MALE aged 21)

In contrast to the perceived relaxing functions for cannabis use, were descriptions by some respondents who felt this drug helped them to concentrate better on certain tasks.

> When I'm on cannabis, I feel I make more conscious decisions, because I can concentrate more . . . I usually have it before I go to work [waitressing], and I enjoy work so much more if I am stoned. (FEMALE aged 19)

Others found it helped them to cope with activities that they found boring or tedious:

Q. You mentioned that you often smoke cannabis to make an everyday activity less boring. What sort of activities do you do this for?

> A. Coming to college! . . . and when I'm at work I smoke. I work weekends. The work I do is

loading [in a factory], and so if you got a buzz then you just feel more happy about doing the work, it makes you feel less tired. Unless I smoke it's boring. (MALE aged 17)

One young man described how he used cannabis to relieve his chronic insomnia as well as to help him to think more clearly:

A. I suffered from insomnia extremely badly when I was younger, and nothing that the doctors told me or gave me would cure the problem. Sleeping pills just knock you out, and then you feel horrible the next day, whereas cannabis really does have a lot of medical uses, one of which is for insomnia.

Q. Is that why you started smoking it?

A. I started smoking it mainly to slow my mind down. My mind would go off at such a horrendous pace that I couldn't actually slow it down enough to use it objectively. I found that under the influence of cannabis it slowed down and I could order my thoughts . . . and I liked the way it made me think. (MALE aged 20)

Amphetamines

The second most commonly used illicit drug by this sample was amphetamines, with 70% having tried them at least once. Use tended to be less frequent than for cannabis. Only four respondents estimated that they had used the drug on over 100 occasions and just over half that they had used it between 20 and 100 times. Amphetamines were perceived as serving a range of functions for respondents in the sample, although these were not as diverse as those for cannabis.

The most commonly cited function for amphetamine use was as an aid to keeping awake and to increase energy levels. The majority of users primarily used the drug at clubs to give them the energy to dance all night. Others used it to give them more confidence, to reduce their inhibitions and even to make them feel more relaxed. The following quote from a 20-year-old female was typical of those who used amphetamines only in nightclubs:

It's [amphetamine use] just for clubbing . . . it keeps me awake, it keeps me going all night, dancing all night, that's why I use it really, and it makes me feel much more happier and relaxed and gets rid of all my inhibitions, and I go for it! (FEMALE aged 20)

Another young female explained how the increased confidence that she experienced from using amphetamines helped her to deal more easily with unpleasant social situations:

I can take anyone being nasty to me if I'm on the speed [amphetamines] . . . otherwise I just burst into tears . . . I'm not a strong person, but I can pretend to be if I'm on speed. (FEMALE aged 21)

The use of amphetamines in situations that were not primarily social was not uncommon, though the functions for use under such circumstances varied. For example, there were reports of using the drug to relieve boredom or tiredness at work or to be more organised at college. The following quotes illustrate these points:

> If anyone asks you to do anything it's not really a problem . . . it's usually when I'm working [waitressing] that I take it [amphetamines]. (FEMALE aged 19)

> I was working at the [large department store] as a Saturday job while I was at college . . . and I spent about £15 [a day] on speed [amphetamines] to keep me going, to make it more enjoyable, because it bored the hell out of me. (21-year-old MALE)

> When I was doing my A levels, I went through a stage of using it [amphetamines] every day, and it's just so good because you're on top of everything. Everything is so organised . . . if someone comes up to you and says, 'Right, I want a 2500-word essay for tomorrow,' and you're like, 'Yeah! Whatever!' and that's why I like it because I'm not an organised person anyway and speed will definitely keep me organised in that respect, and certainly round exam time it is quite handy. (FEMALE aged 18)

Finally, a couple of female respondents mentioned using amphetamines mainly for its appetite-suppressing properties to help them to lose weight. By taking it on the first day of a new diet, they found that they could fast all day, and they reported that this made it easier to eat less on subsequent days.

Ecstasy

Just over half the sample reported that they had tried ecstasy, though four of them had used the drug only once. Forty-eight per cent of these ecstasy users estimated that they had consumed it more than 20 times and a quarter on more than 100 occasions at the time of interview. Ecstasy was generally regarded as a drug whose functions pertained to going out to clubs and parties, though some also used it in other contexts. The reported functions for use were similar in many respects to those for amphetamines, with many users choosing ecstasy to increase their energy for staying up all night and for dancing. Other functions included lowering inhibitions and increasing confidence, thus facilitating social interactions. A few people also described ecstasy as a means of relaxing or 'getting in tune with the music'.

Q. So what are the effects of ecstasy that you like?

> A. I do it when I'm out clubbing. I think it's just the whole euphoric experience you feel – you feel like you want to be having fun. I mean, it just makes me feel like I wanna party, I'm gonna enjoy myself ... and doing drugs like ecstasy gives me a lot more energy as well. (MALE aged 21)

> Es [ecstasy tablets] are just a social thing. With Es the music sounds so good and you are so confident and so open . . . with Es you can sit there quietly and you don't have to talk, you can just sit there and appreciate the music and the company. (FEMALE aged 21)

LSD

Forty-two per cent of the sample reported that they had tried LSD. However, use was much more infrequent than for the other drugs. Nearly half had used on ten occasions or less and only ten (48%) had used LSD in the last year. This figure is noticeably less than that for amphetamines (77%) or ecstasy (85%), and so the available data should be interpreted with caution.

The most commonly reported functions for LSD use included decreasing inhibitions, problem-solving and 'learning more about yourself'. As a 21-year-old male student explained:

> It [LSD] makes me think a lot. It makes me learn about myself more. Each time I take it I learn something new about myself . . . with LSD I tend to sit down and talk and think a lot – it's a nice drug for that. I don't do LSD if I'm at a club or a pub . . . because LSD to me is more of a philosophy drug . . . most of the time we just talk [[rubbish]], but it's meaningful at the time and you do learn something about yourself that you probably didn't know before.

In general, the young people in this sample did not use LSD for clubbing. Respondents felt that they were more likely to lose touch with reality after taking LSD than after ecstasy use and so generally preferred to be somewhere that was safe and predictable when using it. Consequently, for many, using it in quiet, uncrowded places, such as out in the countryside, was preferable to somewhere with a lot of strangers, such as a night-club. Section 6.7 explores this issue further.

Given the potency of the effects of LSD and their duration, the general perception amongst the sample was that 'tripping' on LSD was an activity in itself rather than a means of enhancing or facilitating other activities. It therefore seemed that the principal functions for LSD use were to enjoy the company of friends, to get away from reality or as something to fill time.

Opiates

The majority of the sample had never used any type of opiate. Of the 11 individuals who had, 4 had used only once and a further 3 had used on less than ten occasions. For most, it seemed that use had been purely experimental, and many reported that they had disliked the effects.

However, of those who had used an opiate more frequently, the functions reported for this use clearly differed from those described for the use of other substances. Instead of being used to enhance social activities, opiate use was more often described as a means of escaping from everyday experiences. For example, the following quotes were taken from an interview with an 18-year-old woman who had been sleeping rough for the last nine months. She was a daily cannabis user, used benzodiazepines on occasions to help her to sleep and ecstasy when going to a nightclub. Recently she had begun to inject methadone ampoules, as she had discovered that this drug helped her better to forget her problems and to escape from reality more than cannabis:

> If someone's upset me or I'm in a bad mood, then I'll beg up ten pounds and I'll go and get an amp [ampoule of methadone] . . . but if I'm in quite a jolly mood, then I'll get cannabis.

This young woman had found that using methadone was a more effective means of achieving a positive state of mind than using cannabis.

> An amp [ampoule of methadone] makes you gouch and you forget about everything, because you are so worried about when you are going to be sick next that you just want to be on your own and you just forget about everything . . . I mean cannabis can help because it makes you laugh and so you can sit there and think things are funny, but you know amps block everything out, whereas on cannabis you can still think about it, still think, 'Oh, they really pissed me off,' and then you get a bad buzz with cannabis, whereas with amps, you know what I mean, you just get the same buzz.

Although she also liked using ecstasy, the function that it served for her (increased energy for dancing) was not what she wanted on a day-to-day basis on the street:

Q. If you're going to be sat down all day [on the street] then what would you prefer to use?
> A. I'd rather be on an amp [ampoule of methadone], 'cos that makes you sit down and gouch anyway . . . If I'm on an E and I'm just going to be sitting down all day then there's no point buying it because you're not going to be doing anything. (FEMALE aged 18)

Another respondent (a 21-year-old male) started using heroin when he was homeless because it helped him to feel more confident when shoplifting:

> I started smoking gear [heroin] and I thought it was lovely – brilliant . . . it gave me confidence . . . I used to go out stealing, shoplifting for money – robbing jeans and that – and the gear gave me confidence. I didn't care when I was on that stuff, I thought I was bullet-proof.

More recently he had begun to use other opiates and benzodiazepines, which, despite having pharmacological effects similar to those of heroin, he reported using as a means of escaping from his problems rather than for shoplifting.

Q. So is heroin different to the benzos and the methadone?
> A. Ah, yeah, much different. They just make me sit there and you don't care about nothing, and you basically forget your problems.

Like the 18-year-old female previously quoted, he regarded other drugs, such as stimulants, as serving yet another function:

Q. What about when you've used other things like ecstasy and speed . . . ?
> A. No, that's for socialising. (MALE aged 21)

The two cases quoted above were fairly typical of those from the group of homeless young people who were interviewed. It seemed that their substance use fulfilled very different functions from those reported by the majority of the rest of the sample.

Alcohol

Of all the substances discussed in the interviews, alcohol was reported to serve the most diverse range of functions. This could be linked to the legal status of alcohol, which makes it more widely and easily available than other drugs. Thus, when people have specific needs or functions for engaging in the use of psychoactives, alcohol is often most close to hand and therefore the substance chosen. Alcohol appears to produce quite complex changes in mood, which are influenced by the amount consumed, the setting and context of a drinking occasion. Some respondents used it primarily to decrease their inhibitions or to increase their confidence when socialising. Others reported that they used it to make them feel relaxed, happier and more sociable as well as more inclined to dance when at nightclubs or parties. The following excerpts from the in-depth interviews illustrate some of these functions:

> You feel different, like more up for doing things like dancing in clubs . . . you don't really give a damn, you just do what you want. (FEMALE aged 16)

> I like the Dutch courage bit. You can say a little bit more than what you know you should do and be a bit more daring and a bit more lairy (cheeky). (FEMALE aged 19)

> I get really happy and really nice to everyone. I don't usually get angry with anyone. I think I like it because I'm just happier, a lot happier – hyper. I'm sociable anyway but it gives me more confidence probably. (FEMALE aged 16)

There were also accounts of using alcohol for relieving negative states, such as feeling depressed or bored, as the following quotes suggest:

> It's something to do when you're really bored (FEMALE aged 16)

> I use alcohol for, like, if you're really sort of down . . . you have six or seven pints or something and just be loud and stupid . . . it's just like letting go. (MALE aged 16)

There were frequent reports of using other drugs at the same time as alcohol. Again, there were often clear rationales for this behaviour, with alcohol use having its own distinct function. Issues relating to poly-drug use and concurrent use are discussed in the next few sections of this chapter.

Poly-drug use

For the purposes of this report we have made a distinction between the terms 'poly-drug use' and 'concurrent drug use'. Poly-drug use is used to refer to the patterns of consumption exhibited by people who commonly use several different drugs; concurrent use refers to the use of two or more different substances at the same time.

So far this chapter has focused on the functions reported by the young people we interviewed for their use of individual substances. Each substance has been described as having a range of functions for different individuals, some having similar or even identical uses. For example, when an increase in energy is desired, the user might choose between a number of candidate stimulants, including amphetamines and ecstasy. If wanting something to facilitate relaxation, alcohol or cannabis might be selected. Whilst the choice of substance may hinge on availability, other factors can also be involved in these decision-making processes.

This section examines the choice between amphetamines and ecstasy as an example of how decisions relating to poly-drug use were made by the sample. Half of the sample had tried both of these drugs, yet most reported that, given equal availability, they would definitely choose one over the other. However, although different individuals had different preferences, and often had strict criteria or rules for their first choice, one might be substituted for the other when the preferred drug was unavailable.

For some interviewees their first choice of stimulant, if they were going to a nightclub, would be amphetamines, as the following two quotes illustrate:

> The main thing that I would look for is speed [amphetamines] . . . because it's something that I enjoy taking. So that would be my priority, and I would only take E [ecstasy] if I couldn't get it. (MALE aged 18)

Q. When have you used ecstasy?
>   A. Most times it's been 'cos I haven't been able to get hold of any speed, so I have taken it 'cos one of my friends has offered it to me.

Q. At the moment, if you were going out to a club and you had the choice between speed and ecstasy, how would you make up your mind?
>   A. I'd always go speed first, I think. (FEMALE aged 20)

Two main explanations were offered for why amphetamines were preferable to ecstasy: some indicated that they simply preferred the effects of amphetamines, while others, as shown in the quotes below, thought that using amphetamines was less risky than using ecstasy. However, this opinion did not necessarily deter them from using ecstasy if amphetamines were not easily available.

> I'm not that dead against it [ecstasy] or anything, but I think I'd rather do speed, it just seems to me to be safer. (FEMALE aged 17)

> I think speed and ecstasy are pretty similar, but with speed I don't think there is so much of a risk that you could get a bad tablet or whatever. That's my reasons for why I'd use speed more regularly than I would use Es, because I think that it's safer. (FEMALE aged 20)

Q. Why do you tend to choose speed [amphetamines] over ecstasy?

>A. 'Cos I think Es do frighten me a bit more because of the way it's been advertised more – the stories I've heard . . . I mean speed is probably no better, and it's probably got loads of rubbish in it, but I haven't heard of anyone dying of it, like the stories of E . . . but, having said that, it wouldn't stop me [choosing to use ecstasy] if I hadn't got any speed. (FEMALE aged 20)

Q. Don't you like the pills [ecstasy] so much?

>A. No, I prefer whizz [amphetamines] . . . I just prefer the buzz, I don't know why . . . I can't describe it, I just prefer the feeling. (FEMALE aged 19)

However, for others, their first choice of stimulant was definitely ecstasy. Amphetamines would only be substituted if this drug was unavailable.

Q. Do you use speed [amphetamines] at clubs now?

>A. If I can't get hold of any ecstasy, I'll do speed and drink beer. (MALE aged 21)

Q. If you can't get a pill, would you choose speed?

>A. If it wasn't really readily available, I suppose I'd plump for it in the end, just for the fact that I know that I could drink and I wouldn't get as drunk and it would just keep me up all night. (MALE aged 20)

Those who preferred using ecstasy rather than amphetamines often cited the 'come-down' (the period when the effects of stimulants begin to wear off) as the major factor which influenced this choice. These individuals reported that they felt much worse the day after taking amphetamines than after ecstasy. As an 18-year-old female explained:

>My friends sometimes do some speed, but I don't like it so I don't do it. I don't like the comedown . . . it's such a [[bad]] comedown that it's not worth the buzz. The buzz isn't that good. I mean it's good, but it's not worth the comedown . . . On Es the comedown's [[bad]] but it's not as [[bad]] as the speed comedown and the buzz is better than the speed buzz. (FEMALE aged 18)

Nevertheless, this opinion was by no means universal, as others reported little or no experience of 'bad comedowns' from amphetamines:

>I've never had any problems on speed, I've never had a bad comedown . . . never been paranoid . . . I've never had a problem on it, so it's going to be a drug that I would widely use again if any. It's one which I enjoy taking . . . it keeps me awake, keeps me buzzing for the night, and it keeps me happy. (MALE aged 18)

Concurrent drug use

The use of more than one substance at the same time was not uncommon amongst this sample of young people. Similar patterns of concurrent drug use have been reported in other studies of young drug users (e.g. Boys, Lenton & Norcross 1997). However, this study was not primarily concerned with documenting patterns of concurrent use in detail. Instead the aim was to try to identify factors that influenced decisions to use a particular substance whilst already experiencing the effects of another.

Many of those interviewed explained that the main function of using additional substances was to help to manage the effects of other drugs. Use of cannabis for this purpose was popular, particularly in combination with amphetamines, ecstasy or LSD. As a 20-year-old male explained, cannabis might be used to help manage the initial effects from a drug such as ecstasy:

> We'll always smoke dope [cannabis] before we take ecstasy, but small quantities because it puts you in that mood and you're less likely to come up too fast [experience the initial effects from the ecstasy tablet too strongly] and freak yourself out. (MALE aged 20)

There were also reports of using cannabis when the effects of a substance began to wear off, as the following quote from his 21-year-old friend illustrates:

> I use cannabis just basically to slow me down. I mean I usually use cannabis as I'm coming down off my drug [ecstasy, cocaine or LSD]. I mean instead of coming just whack, bang, [[. . . . . .]], straight down, cannabis usually kind of floats me down. (MALE aged 21)

Some respondents used alcohol in similar circumstances to manage or enhance the effects from such drugs as ecstasy or cannabis. A few examples of this type of use follow:

> We generally drink before we take ecstasy as it [alcohol] does help to relax you. (MALE aged 20)

> The only time I have half a lager is because it gives me a kick [helps her to get high] when I'm on a pill [ecstasy]. (FEMALE aged 21)

> I went through a phase of drinking and smoking [cannabis] as well, just because I'd get more out of smoking by drinking a load . . . because it would make the high better. (MALE aged 21)

There was less evidence that other substances were used to help manage drug effects. However, some described using amphetamines to help reduce feelings of drunkenness and therefore increase their ability to continue drinking alcohol throughout an evening.

> If I can't get hold of any ecstasy, I'll do speed and drink beer, 'cos with speed, when I do use speed at clubs, I find that I can drink a hell of a lot more . . . which is quite fun, but it's no good on my wallet! (MALE aged 21)

Q. So, about how much do you usually drink?

> A. Probably about eight pints in total and then I know that I'm pretty gone, and then once I take a bit of speed I know that I'm just happy really and mellow and know that I'll have a good evening. (MALE aged 18)

6.2 Expectancies

In addition to the functions for substance use, an individual's beliefs (or expectancies) concerning the effects of a drug may also influence the substance-related decisions that they make. For example, if they wanted something to help them to stay up late to write an essay (the function for the use), they would need to choose a substance which they believed would help them to stay awake but would not interfere with their concentration (the expectancies of the drug effects). As mentioned in the introduction, research over the last decade has examined expectancies for alcohol (Carey 1995) and cocaine (Jaffe & Kilbey 1994), but there is little available literature on the predictive value of expectancies concerning other psychoactive substances. The relationship between function and expectancy is complicated, as these expectancies are likely to exert complex influences on an individual's reactions to a substance. For example, the vascular stimulation effects of amphetamines (e.g. increased heart rate) may be perceived negatively as anxiety. This could increase the probability that the effects of amphetamines will be considered uncomfortable on the next occasion of use.

The data from this study supported these ideas. Users tended to report that they preferred to use drugs with stimulant properties when they were going out to a club or wanting to stay up all night. In contrast to this, drugs such as cannabis were generally used for functions such as facilitating relaxation and encouraging sleep. An individual's personal rating of their expectancies of a drug's effects was also important. If they had disliked an experience with a drug, then they were likely to expect a similar experience on the next occasion of use and were thus more likely to decide against subsequent use. The following quote from an interview with a 21-year-old male illustrates this point:

> I'd never take acid [LSD] again or any strong hallucinogen . . . 'cos it just [[messes]] my head up . . . makes me paranoid. I lose myself completely in it, it completely takes control over me.
> (MALE aged 21)

There was also some evidence that expectancies concerning both the immediate and the long-term consequences of using a drug could affect the current intensity and frequency of use, as another male respondent explained:

> It's not just the short-term consequences, but long-term consequences too, how much you're spending on it, how much it's affecting, say, going out and stuff. I mean, if you sit in and smoke pot every night of the week, you're not going to go out and meet people, you're not going to keep up a big circle of friends, you're just going to drop out of society. (MALE aged 20)

The sources of expectancies varied: some were based on hearsay and some on personal experience, while others had resulted from observing peers. The following excerpt from an interview with a 21-year-old male suggests that he had a good idea of what to expect from ecstasy before trying it for the first time:

> Well, I did know what the effects were, because a lot of my friends at the time were already into the rave scene . . . I was into the rave scene, but I was just doing speed, just to keep me going, and, by the time I actually got round to using ecstasy, I'd already seen what ecstasy was doing . . . what it did to other people. (MALE aged 21)

By observing her friends, one of the 16-year-old females had learnt that cannabis could affect individuals very differently:

> A. I don't think there's much I do like about smoking dope. I suppose from my friends I see it affects people really differently . . . one of the boys goes really dopey and doesn't say anything and the other one gets really hyper and cheerful, and there's the one who's just really annoying and does annoying things.

Q. What about the girls?

> A. All my friends, because they don't smoke it too often, they just get really giggly, and that's funny. (FEMALE aged 16)

Another female respondent (aged 21) had never tried LSD herself but had seen several friends under the influence of it.

> They just sit in a corner and look all weird for ages and start chatting to themselves . . . You wonder why I don't want to take it? I've seen the state of my friends!

These observations had affected her expectancies about the effects of LSD and led to the conclusion that she would not like to experience this particular drug.

> I just couldn't imagine controlling something like that . . . I mean you can't stop it once it starts and it lasts a long time, like eight to twelve hours. (FEMALE aged 21)

As an individual gathers more experience or information about a drug, their expectancies may become more sophisticated. For example, an initial expectation about the effects from cannabis could be 'cannabis makes me giggly', but, as more experience is gathered by watching people, listening to stories or from increased personal use, this expectancy might be modified to take dosage into account, thus becoming 'cannabis makes me giggly if I smoke a little and very dopey if I smoke a lot'. With the addition of another substance, such as alcohol, a further modification could be: 'cannabis makes me giggly if I smoke a little and very dopey if I smoke a lot. But if I smoke cannabis after I've been drinking alcohol, then I get sick.'

Another variable which may gradually be incorporated into the drug-related expectancies held by an individual is their current state. This could be on a physical level (such as feeling tired) or a psychological level (such as feeling depressed). The next section examines the data in which respondents referred to their current state and how this impacted on their drug-related decision-making.

6.3 Current physical or psychological state

Some respondents described how their current physical or psychological state could affect what they expected the effects of drug or alcohol use would be. On occasions this seemed to be a crucial influence on the decision whether or not to use a substance at that particular time. For example, one experienced user of LSD explained how he thought a user's current psychological state could have an impact on the effects experienced from this drug:

> I always stop people from taking it [LSD] when I'm with them if they've got problems at that time, 'cos . . . if you're dwelling on something that's depressing you, all the emotions that you've bottled up do come out on LSD. (MALE aged 20)

Another male respondent explained how his current mood and environment might affect whether or not he decided to try a new substance:

> If I'm in a good mood, if I'm not feeling depressed, if I'm happy with the way I am for the minute, and if I'm in a room full of friends that I'm close enough to be able to say, 'Look, I'm going to be sick, is it all right if [[I'm sick]] in your bathroom?' you know I might. (MALE aged 21)

He went on to explain how the drug and alcohol-related choices that he makes on a regular basis are influenced by his current state. This particular user seemed to have clear set rules and boundaries concerning his substance use, which were designed to insulate him from the risk of developing drug-related problems. In the following excerpt he explains this further:

> A. I never do drugs to cheer myself up. I will smoke cannabis to calm myself down, but if I'm feeling depressed then I will never do ecstasy . . . I will never do speed or LSD or anything in order to cheer myself up. I'll only ever do it if I'm already happy.

Q. Why won't you do it to cheer yourself up?

> A. Because that's what I see as then becoming psychologically dependent on the drug, because if you do it once, obviously next time it happens then you'll just go, 'Oh, I'll do it again,' and then you'll do it again and again and again, and that's how addiction would overtake me . . . but if I make sure that I'm happy and relaxed and everything before I take the drug, then I know that it's not the drug that's making me happy, it's me that's making me happy and it's just the drug that's making it better! And therefore I don't feel any dependence on the drug. (MALE aged 21)

In addition to their current psychological state, some participants in the study also mentioned that their physical state influenced their drug and alcohol-related decisions. For example, they might consider how tired they were or if they were already feeling the effects from another substance. A 20-year-old male explained how he and his friends rarely used ecstasy if they were already feeling the effects from alcohol:

> We very rarely take ecstasy when we go out drinking . . . If you take ecstasy when you are really pissed, it can reduce the effects of ecstasy. When you take ecstasy, you've got to be alive and awake, 'cos all you're gonna want to do is run around and be active . . . you don't want to be tranquillised out on something like alcohol. It's basically just to make full use of it, to get the best effects. (MALE aged 20)

6.4 Gender differences

Data from the 1990 HEA's survey of 16–19-year-olds suggested that experimentation with drugs was more prevalent amongst young males than females (HEA/MORI 1992). Similar findings were reported in other UK and international studies conducted in the early 1990s (Mott & Mirrlees-Black 1995; Johnston, O'Malley & Bachman 1995). However, in subsequent surveys this inequality has been less apparent, with the most recent HEA survey finding little difference between the sexes in the prevalence of drug use (HEA/BMRB International 1997). Nevertheless, there is some evidence that the types of drugs used may differ between the sexes.

In order to explore this issue, participants were asked whether they thought there were any differences in how the males and females in their social groups used drugs and alcohol. In general, the only consistent differences reported were in the quantities consumed: males tended to drink more alcohol than females and smoke more cannabis on a typical using occasion. However there did not appear to be a general consensus that males actually typically got more 'drunk' or more 'stoned' than the females. Two further points were made. Amongst the younger respondents (16- and 17-year-olds) our data suggest that the females in the sample drank more heavily than the males, who preferred to smoke cannabis instead. One possible explanation for this may be that females of this age tend to look older and can therefore purchase alcohol more easily than males of the same age. Another possible suggestion could be that boys of that age are more likely to commit illegal acts, such as using illicit drugs. The explanation suggested by some of the younger respondents was that the effects of cannabis appeal more to males and that alcohol appeals more to females, as the following quotes illustrate:

A. Oh yeah! The girls drink a lot more . . . a lot, lot more! All the girls we hang around with will out-drink any of the boys, which is not usual really . . . .but that's just 'cos we smoke instead.

Q. Is that the reason, because you smoke cannabis and they drink?

A. Yeah, I mean, they puff [smoke cannabis] as well, but it's not really their sort of thing . . . a lot of girls just don't like the feeling of it as well, 'cos girls around boys normally get quite anxious anyway, 'cos they're worried about their appearance and all that and on draw as well it's even worse 'prang' [paranoia], whereas on beer and alcohol they can be loud and they don't really care. I think it just works better for girls that way, because they do get intimidated by boys . . . unless they've got a strong sort of personality, they don't smoke so much draw. (MALE aged 16)

In contrast to the above quote, a female of the same age explained these differences as being due to the boys being unable to 'handle' alcohol.

Q. What about the boys? Do you think there's any difference from the girls?

A. They don't drink half as much . . . they actually don't drink much at all.

Q. Why?

> A. 'Cos they're mostly into draw and they can't handle it [alcohol]. They seem to get ill quicker than the girls. They try and show off drinking a lot at one time and then get and make fools of themselves. So, they don't do it as much in front of us. (FEMALE aged 16)

Similar suggestions were made by the older respondents: males and females look for different types of effects from drugs, the females preferring physical effects, such as an increase in energy, the males hallucinations or perceptual distortions. This is illustrated in the following excerpts:

> A. Girls tend to like speed more because it's a totally physical thing. It just wakes you up, makes you do more stuff and it doesn't affect your mind in any way. Girls don't like more of the psychoactive drugs like acid . . . a lot of girls wouldn't take acid because it just messes with your head too much.

Q. Why do you think they don't like that?

> A. I don't know, perhaps they're just more sensible! I think at the end of the day they just prefer to be more in control. I don't mind being in a situation where I don't know what I'm doing, I don't know what's going on and I've totally lost it and I get all confused . . . but I think it might worry them. (male aged 20)

Another male of the same age had similar opinions:

Q. Do you think there are any differences in how males and females use drugs or alcohol?

> A. Definitely – in quantity and reason and types . . . women are more cautious and will take less than men. Women generally like to stay in control a lot more and tend to stay away from drugs like LSD, and don't take it in anywhere near the amounts that we take it in, simply because they don't like the feeling of being completely out of control. I think women are generally less interested in pushing it to the limits . . . they'd rather stay within the bounds of safety. (MALE aged 20)

6.5 Commitments

An individual's role-responsibilities or commitments in society were also identified as influential on the substance-related decisions made. They may limit the amount of a particular substance that they consume or the timing when consumption takes place in order to ensure that they can perform effectively in their role. Although most young people do not have the responsibilities that adulthood brings, they are not necessarily without commitments.

Respondents were asked if having to do something later that day or the next day would influence the decisions they made concerning drug or alcohol use. Their responses clearly indicated that commitments were frequently considered when deciding on the types and quantities of drugs or alcohol to consume. However, whilst for some individuals this factor had a major influence over their choices, for others the effect was minimal.

Respondents tended to limit use of the drug types with longer-acting effects because of commitments. Although substances such as cannabis and alcohol were used routinely, this was often in smaller quantities in these circumstances. For example, several participants reported that they had recently cut down on their cannabis use during the week, as they found that it made them lethargic and less likely to get things done at college or work.

Some reported that if they had a commitment the next day they would not consume any psychoactive substances the previous evening:

Q. If you're drinking a lot or using speed, do you think about what you've got to do the next day?

> A. I suppose so, like, if I was working really early then I don't think I'd do it. But if, like, it was a Sunday, I wouldn't really care, 'cos I could just sleep all day. (FEMALE aged 18)

A female student nurse (aged 21) claimed that if she had college work to do she would try not to go out in the evening but did not always stick to this resolution. However, she maintained that she would definitely abstain from drug use during the previous night if she was working on a ward the following day.

Other commitments that were mentioned by respondents included playing football, taking exams, starting college or going to work. As a 21-year-old male chef explained:

> If I'm going to go out and get myself into such a state that I am not able to work properly the next day, then I will make sure that the next day is a day off. I'll plan ahead, because being a chef you've got to be at least ninety-eight per cent together, because a kitchen is an extremely dangerous place. (MALE aged 21).

Some respondents reported that if they had commitments the following day, there were certain measures they would take in order to manage the after-effects from their drug use. For example, one male (aged 18) said that he would still use drugs but would make sure that he had a good night's sleep afterwards in order to recover:

Q. Would you worry about commitments the next day?

> A. I normally know a sort of time limit of when to take it [a drug], so if I know that there is something on for the next day, then I need my sleep. So, if I was taking anything, then I know the average hours that most drugs last, so I would consume them so many hours before I was going to go to bed so that I knew that by the time I got home the effects would be wearing off.

Q. So, if you're making a calculation about taking something so that you have enough time to sleep, what's 'enough time'?

> A. About seven hours. (MALE aged 18)

Others suggested that they would be more likely to choose certain types of drugs if they knew that they had to get up the following morning. For example, a 21-year-old male reported that after taking amphetamines he often felt 'groggy' or depressed for two or three days. In contrast, he felt 'fine' after taking ecstasy, and felt 'great' on a morning following cocaine use. He went on to explain how he would decide between different drug types during an evening out with friends:

Q. Does how you feel afterwards affect how you decide what you are going to use?

A. Yeah, depending on if I have things to do the next day, then I'd probably choose ecstasy, 'cos I can come down quite easily on that . . . if I could afford coke, then I'd have that. (MALE aged 21)

However, as is illustrated in Section 6.1 on 'functions', work commitments do not always preclude substance use. Indeed, some individuals reported using drugs specifically for work, in order to combat boredom or to increase their energy levels.

6.6 Boundaries

Ideas of what behaviours are acceptable and what are not can vary widely amongst young people. Similarly, individuals have different 'boundaries' which delineate the extent of their substance use. Groups of friends often share common beliefs, values and ideas, and these help to form part of the cohesive forces which hold them together. A section of the qualitative interview explored the boundaries set by peer groups regarding substance use and how these affected their drug and alcohol-related decisions.

Crack cocaine was regarded as unacceptable by virtually everyone interviewed. Just two individuals had tried this form of cocaine: both were part of a group of respondents who were experiencing extreme social problems such as homelessness. The rest of the sample overwhelmingly reported that they and their peers regarded it as very addictive and dangerous. Similar views were expressed towards heroin, as the following quotes illustrate:

I've heard a lot about it [crack] that it's really really addictive and . . . although I say that I could try something and not go back to it . . . I don't know . . . I mean I'd probably try heroin – I dare say in the future I will try it – but I won't inject. (MALE aged 20)

They [her friends] wouldn't take crack cocaine either. I think that's because of the reputation it's got and because it's so addictive . . . I think it's a destructive drug like heroin as well. Although most drugs affect your personality, from experience I think that crack and heroin do much more. (FEMALE aged 19)

The use of cocaine powder was often perceived by the less experienced drug users as equally unacceptable. In contrast, some of the older, more experienced respondents seemed to regard it as completely different from using crack. Most of the 14 respondents who had used cocaine powder, but not crack, described how they perceived cocaine to be much more dangerous in the form of crack. One such person was a 21-year-old male who had had considerable experience with illicit drugs (had used LSD, ecstasy and cannabis very extensively and had tried heroin). The following excerpt summarises his attitudes towards crack use:

It [crack] scares me . . . there's not much talked about it, not much anyone hears about it apart from the fact that you can get addicted to it very easily . . . and it's kind of socially unacceptable. (MALE aged 21)

Even those with considerable substance use experience (which might seem unacceptable to many of the sample group) had their own boundaries, indicating what they would or would not do. For example, another 21-year-old male, whose friends were fairly regular heavy drug users (cannabis, ecstasy, amphetamines, LSD, magic mushrooms, ketamine, valium, and a few using heroin) described how he perceived the boundaries held by his peer group.

Q. Do your friends use cocaine [powder]?

    A. No. A lot of them would like to, but you don't get much coke in Devon!

Q. What about crack?

    A. No I don't think anybody would . . . well, I say that, but probably the odd person who takes heroin would do crack, but all the other people wouldn't . . . because as far as me and ninety-nine point nine per cent of my friends are concerned, you get so far and then there's a line, and then across that line is heroin and crack and stuff, the things that you just don't do because they are too strong for people to handle and shouldn't be touched.

Q. So you'd put crack on that side of the line. Would they also put cocaine powder on that side of the line?

    A. No. (MALE aged 21)

The other drug that was viewed as socially unacceptable by most respondents was heroin. With very few exceptions, when respondents were asked which drugs they thought that their peer group would never use, heroin was most commonly cited. Some also mentioned that drug use by injection was something that their friends would never try. Several of the respondents had tried smoking heroin and these vehemently asserted that they would never consider injecting it, most indicating that they did not think that they would use the drug again anyway, perpetuating at least part of this common boundary. The few who reported that they had tried it and had also injected it or another opiate (3, 6.0%) were still of the opinion that most of their peer group did not find it acceptable. These views are illustrated in the following excerpts:

Q. Are there any drugs you and your friends would never use?

    A. Heroin, and I don't think any of my friends would ever inject.

Q. Why?

    A. I think heroin is very expensive, isn't it, and I just think that generally we're not all big massive drug users. I don't think we abuse them, I don't think that any of us are addicted, and I think that heroin is that thing that you can get addicted to and is more likely to kill you, and is something that people use or abuse on a regular basis once you start taking it. I think that they can't stop. (FEMALE aged 20)

Another 20-year-old female explained how her peer group had definitely affected where her drug-related boundaries lay.

It seems OK to take Es and speed and things but wrong to take heroin. I think that's from my social circle. (FEMALE aged 20)

Those in the sample who mainly used alcohol and cannabis and had had very little experience of other drug use often reported that they and their peers grouped drugs such as ecstasy alongside heroin and crack:

Q. Are there any drugs that you think your friends would never use or try?

    A. Most of my friends probably wouldn't use heroin, and a lot of them wouldn't try ecstasy.

Q. Why?

    A. Because we've heard about people dying. It's too dangerous, they don't want to risk it. They're put off by the idea of injecting drugs as well. (FEMALE aged 16)

The remainder of this chapter examines the social-contextual factors which were identified as influencing the drug and alcohol-related decisions made by the sample.

6.7 Environment

The importance of the 'setting' in which substance use takes place has been discussed in detail by Zinberg (1984). The immediate environment may have significant impact on the effects that an individual experiences from a substance. This section explores how our sample of young people felt that environmental factors influenced their drug and alcohol-related decisions.

A few respondents reported that they had decided against using a substance for the first time because they felt that the environment was unsuitable. For example, one of the 16-year-old male respondents had had the opportunity to use magic mushrooms when he was at a friend's house. However, he had decided against it because he was going to be driven home and did not want to be under the influence of the drug whilst in the car.

Several talked about needing to be in the 'right sort of place' when using certain drugs, particularly those with hallucinogenic effects. Although opinions were by no means uniform, there were clear opinions on the kind of environment or context perceived by the sample as suitable for using certain substances. Cannabis was not only the most commonly used illicit drug amongst this sample, it was also the drug used in the widest range of circumstances. Although it was generally smoked in social groups at friend's houses, some respondents also used it at nightclubs. However, there was some suggestion that a nightclub was not an ideal environment for heavy use of cannabis, as the effects reported by most (relaxation and drowsiness) were not conducive to dancing all night. Those who used cannabis under these circumstances tended to report that they deliberately moderated their use on these occasions. This is illustrated by the following quotes:

I will have some [cannabis] after [clubs] but not before . . . because you don't feel like dancing when you're smoking pot. You just feel like sitting there and going to sleep. (MALE aged 16)

I don't go out to a club and smoke loads of cannabis because the effects aren't very nice when you're at a club, 'cos you want to be able to fall asleep, so it's usually at friends' houses . . . I smoke a bit at a club, but not enough to get really wasted. (FEMALE aged 19)

Although using LSD in a club-type environment was not unknown, most users reported that they preferred to use it under less crowded, more predictable circumstances. This seemed to be due to concerns that users might experience anxious or 'paranoid' thoughts or otherwise get themselves into trouble.

Q. When do you use LSD?

A. Well, usually that would be at someone's house or out in the countryside, because it's away from civilisation and you've not got any of the stresses.

Q. Would you use it in a club?

A. I don't know . . . if you use a lot, you aren't in touch with reality anymore. You don't know what's going on at all and you just sit back and watch the pretty pictures. So I wouldn't take a lot in a club because, at the end of the day, you don't know . . . if you are in a social place then you do have to be in touch with reality to sort of handle yourself in those sorts of situation because you don't know what's going to happen. I mean you might end up in some kind of trouble. (MALE aged 20)

Another male respondent had similar opinions:

I would never want to be in a club [when using LSD] because of the paranoid side of it. I'd rather be round a friend's house and all of us take it. I would not like to take it on my own. I'd want everyone to be using the same drug and experiencing the same kind of thing as I would . . . Yeah, I'd rather be in someone's house or sitting in a field, lying down or watching the world go by. (MALE aged 18)

So did a female respondent of the same age:

I'd never do it [LSD] in a club, it would be too much, too sort of hectic . . . I think to do it you have to be with people you know really well and in a wide open space . . . the best place I did it was on a beach. (FEMALE aged 18)

Some also mentioned that whilst under the influence of LSD, they would prefer to avoid contact with other people who had been drinking heavily.

If we're going to get off our heads [under the influence of LSD], it's a whole lot safer doing it out of the city, then you're not likely to walk into some of the dickheads you get round here who go out looking for trouble. So we prefer to avoid that or go to people's houses . . . especially if we're gonna take something like LSD. You don't know what you're doing, especially if you come across someone who's been drinking and is really lairy. (MALE aged 20)

For most, the use of ecstasy was firmly linked with going out to nightclubs. Many had strong opinions as to what type of nightclub was suitable, and similar sentiments to those described by LSD users were expressed concerning interactions with people who had been drinking heavily. This was further explained by the 20-year-old male quoted above:

> A. Some clubs are more geared towards the use of E, the dance clubs [for instance]. If you're going to take ecstasy, then you go to a dance club, 'cos you have a whole better night out . . . plus the atmosphere at dance clubs is nicer. People are generally a lot friendlier to each other and you get a good vibe, whereas if you do an E in a club where people are drinking, the atmosphere is totally different . . . there's aggravation in the air and people are sitting there with their ego hats on and act like idiots. (MALE aged 20)

Q. So do you adjust what you use according to the type of club you are in?

> A. Yeah. If we feel like going out drinking, we'll go to a club that sells cheap beer . . . people just go there to drink, basically . . . we very rarely take ecstasy when we go out drinking.

A 21-year-old male was of a similar opinion:

Q. Any situations you'd avoid on ecstasy?

> A. Lager louts. I avoid lager louts like the plague when I'm on ecstasy, like [I do] when I'm on acid . . . it's that whole stereotype about lager louts . . . it's like I really don't want to be facing a drunken sod tonight in the state of mind I'm in . . . 'cos on drugs you might innocently say the wrong word . . . [and] if you say it to a lager lout they'll probably take it the wrong way. (MALE aged 21)

6.8 Availability

Measures to reduce the supply of certain drugs and tackling the drug markets are the cornerstone of national and international drug policy. On the individual level, whilst the availability of a drug is obviously necessary, it is not in itself a sufficient condition for use to occur. An individual may choose to abstain from an available drug, or choose an alternative substance. Availability is widely considered to be one of the most important contextual factors that influences whether or not someone decides to use a drug: furthermore it is the one factor that could outweigh all others in determining whether or not a substance is consumed. However, this is not necessarily a clear-cut, binary condition. The relative ease with which a substance can be obtained (i.e. how much it costs the individual to obtain it in time, inconvenience, etc.) will also influence a decision whether or not to use it.

The data from this study suggest that if the drug of preference is not available to an individual, then this does not necessarily mean that they will abstain from substance use on that particular occasion (see Section 6.1, p. 24). Instead respondents often reported that they would choose an alternative substance on occasions when the first choice of drug was unavailable. This is illustrated in the following excerpts.

I only use speed in . . . dire emergencies when I really feel like doing some drugs and there's nothing around. (FEMALE aged 18)

Q. What about ecstasy? When have you used that?

A. I used it in a club once, when funnily enough I couldn't get any speed before I went . . . I went in there, the dealer didn't have any speed, he only had Es . . . so I took half with a friend . . .

Q. So, the times when you've used ecstasy . . .

A. Most times it's been 'cos I haven't been able to get hold of any speed. (FEMALE aged 20)

Others reported that in extreme circumstances, when amphetamines were unavailable, they would resort to over-the-counter high-dose caffeine preparations such as 'Pro-plus'.

Q. Do you know people who use Pro-plus when they 'go out'?

A. I used to, 'cos it's better than speed, well, not better, but as in safer and cleaner. It's just caffeine.

Q. So it was an alternative to speed?

A. Yeah, well, it was probably at that time more to do with the fact we couldn't get any. (MALE aged 20)

Q. Have you ever used Pro-plus?

A. When we were on holiday, then we used it . . . with drink . . . we couldn't get anything out there and – just like in place of speed.

Q. How much did you have?

A. About six tablets [at a time].

Q. Did it work?

Not so much. It just made you feel like you had loads of energy really, but not nearly as much as speed. (FEMALE aged 18)

There was also some evidence that a lack of availability of some drugs (often cannabis) had prompted initiation into the use of other drug types. For example, in the following quote, a male aged 20 explains how he first came to try amphetamines:

The first time I took speed – I was about sixteen – was when I couldn't get any cannabis . . . [We] couldn't get any cannabis while we were in the pub . . . so we were offered some speed and so we took it and that was the first time that I tried it . . . same with ecstasy. First time I took ecstasy was 'cos there was no cannabis on the market. (MALE aged 20)

Another male respondent (aged 21) took LSD for the first time under similar circumstances:

A. The first time I took acid I was in a pub and I was trying to get some hash [cannabis] . . . and I couldn't get hold of any hash, and then someone said to me, 'Do you take acid?' and I said, 'Why not? OK.' (This was when I was sixteen.)

Q. Did you know what to expect?

> A. I had no idea, no idea . . . and I thought it was brilliant! (MALE aged 21)

This experience had a major effect on him and he immediately started to use LSD quite heavily. Then, a few months later, when he was unable to find any LSD, he was offered ecstasy instead:

> A. The first time I ever took an E, I was looking for some acid and I couldn't get any, and somebody said to me, 'Do you ever do Es?' and I said, 'No,' and he said, 'Do you want to?' . . . 'Yeah, all right!'

Q. But it's quite a different price, isn't it?

> A. Yeah, but at the time I was being really ripped off on acid and paying like five pounds for a trip, and so twelve pounds for an E wasn't that much more, and anyway there was definitely no chance of getting any acid and so it was that or nothing. (MALE aged 21)

It seems that when these young people wanted to obtain specific drugs for a specific purpose and found their drug of choice was unavailable, they were motivated to find an alternative substance to fulfil the purpose. In some cases, such as for the 21-year-old quoted above, this occasion was a significant milestone in their drug-using careers.

The availability of certain illicit drugs not only seemed to influence whether individuals chose to use them or not, but also influenced the intensity and frequency of their use. As a 20-year-old male explained:

Q. What do you think have been the major influences on your use of speed since you first tried it?

> A. I think the biggest influence has probably been availability . . . because when you're at that sort of age – seventeen or eighteen – if you can get it, you'll have it, because you don't think about the consequences much. I mean, if I had stumbled across a dealer I would have ended up in a right state probably. (MALE aged 20)

One 19-year-old female described a time a few years earlier when she had used amphetamines much more regularly than she was at the time of the interview:

> When I was sixteen I used to live in a dealer's house, and for about a year and a half I was constantly taking it. I mean not every single day, but the majority of days, because I didn't have to pay for it and it was there on a plate for me . . . (FEMALE aged 19)

Finally, there was some evidence that respondents had made rules for themselves that governed their sources of illicit drugs. They preferred to purchase from a known individual instead of from a stranger, particularly if in a nightclub. If their drug of choice was not available from these trusted sources, they might decide to abstain from use on that occasion:

Q. So do you get it [amphetamines] off friends or from a dealer?

> A. I get it off a friend . . . I never want to walk into a club and get it off a dealer . . . (FEMALE aged 20)

Q. So do you get your drugs before you go to a club?

> A. Yeah, yeah, I wouldn't buy anything from a dodgy club dealer. (MALE aged 21)

There was also evidence that some of the sample took positive measures to limit their access to certain drugs. For example, one of the male respondents reported that he would definitely like to try heroin, but would not like to know where to get it, because he was afraid that this could increase the temptation to use on future occasions:

> I know people who have it [heroin], but I've never actually gone out looking for the drug . . . it's something I wouldn't want to do . . . if I knew someone who sold heroin then the temptation for me to go back and get the drug a second time would probably be a bit too great . . . so if I was to try it, it would have to be from a source where I didn't know where it came from. (MALE aged 20)

6.9 Finances

Drugs and alcohol can be regarded as belonging to a range of consumable items upon which young people spend their money. The amount of disposable income an individual has is likely to strongly affect whether or not they choose to purchase and use these commodities. This was not a matter of concern for those amongst the sample whose partners or friends supplied them with psychoactive substances free of charge, but, for the majority, money played an important part in their decision-making processes in respect of drug use. This section examines the role that drugs and alcohol had within the overall range of consumable items that our sample spent their money on and how the amount of income that they had affected their substance-related decisions.

There was huge variation in the amount of disposable income reported by the sample (disposable income was defined as any money that was spare after paying rent and bills). Estimates ranged from £14 per week (a 16-year-old female, living with her parents) to £420 per week (a homeless 17-year-old male making money from petty crime and begging). The average weekly disposable income for the sample was £75 (median = £50).

How this money was spent also varied. Table 6.1 summarises the average amount that respondents estimated spending on each of six items per month (clothes, records/CDs, entrance fees to clubs, cigarettes, alcohol and other drugs). In order to examine how money was prioritised by the interviewees, these figures were used to calculate a percentage of overall monthly disposable income spent on each commodity. Thus someone who has £200 of disposable income per month and spends £100 per month on cigarettes would score 50, indicating that 50% of their disposable income is spent on cigarettes.

Table 6.1 Monthly expenditure on different consumable items

	Number	Monthly expenditure		% of disposable income	
		Range (£)	Average (£)	Range	Average
Cigarettes	39	4–180	53	1–83	26
Alcohol	40	5–360	72	1–100+	32
Other drugs	36	7–3000	94	1–100+	36
Clothes/ shoes	41	5–400	85	6–100+	35
Records/CDs	27	5–50	17	2–42	9
Club entrance	36	4–120	27	3–25	11

Note: 'Disposable income' was defined as money in excess of that which was needed to pay for accommodation and bills.

The *n* values in the left-hand column differ, as some participants reported that in a 'typical' month they did not spend anything on certain items. For a minority this was because clothes were bought for them by their parents and alcohol by friends or they paid for drugs through small-scale dealing. Therefore, it cannot be assumed that an individual who reported not spending any of their disposable income on the above commodities was not a consumer of these items. Thus averages shown in Table 6.1 are the mean amount spent per month by those who spent *something* on this item. When interpreting the data, the number who did not typically spend anything on an item should also be considered.

The observation that several interviewees reported spending more than 100% of their disposable income on alcohol, drugs and clothes has several possible explanations. Firstly, many of the participants were students, were therefore on low incomes and also probably borrowing money in the form of bank overdrafts or student loans. Secondly, a few of the respondents had illicit sources of money, such as drug dealing, other petty crimes or begging. This type of income is usually irregular in nature and may not have been included in their estimated monthly disposable income. Finally, some of the interviewees indicated that although they usually bought their own clothes, their parents often reimbursed them for these items.

It seems that this sample of young people spent an amount on clothes very similar to that spent on alcohol and on other drugs. This suggests that equal or greater priority was given to psychoactive substances relative to more essential consumer durables. If the amounts spent on cigarettes, alcohol and other drugs are added together for each person and once again expressed as a percentage of their overall disposable income, the following observations can be made: The average amount spent on these items per month was £154 (range 0–402). Alternatively, it can be said that, on average, most respondents estimated that they spent at least half (59%) of their disposable income on these substances. These figures suggest that psychoactive substances were generally prioritised over and above music or buying extra clothes for the young people interviewed in this sample.

During the in-depth, qualitative part of the interview, we asked respondents to explain in more detail how they prioritised their spending. In general people tended to describe items connected with socialising, such as alcohol, drugs and paying to get into night-clubs, as most important, although some of the younger female respondents also some-times reported prioritising clothes or make-up, as the following excerpts illustrate:

Q. If you've got a certain amount of money, what are the most important things to spend it on? Is it going out, alcohol, clothes or what?

A. Clothes will come first and then alcohol and then going out, and that's about all I do spend my money on.

Q. What about cigarettes?

A. Oh yeah . . . I usually have loose change in the bottom of my bag and that's what I spend it on. I don't really think about spending money on cigarettes, it's just that I always seem to buy them! (FEMALE aged 16)

Her friend had similar priorities:

Q. How do you prioritise your money?

A. It depends on what I need at the time. If I need a top or something for a party I'd probably buy that. If I didn't need any clothes or make-up or anything I'd probably spend it on alcohol or something like that.

Q. Would cannabis come after alcohol?

A. Yeah, I'm more likely to buy alcohol. (FEMALE aged 16)

Many of the interviewees had left home and were therefore responsible for paying their own rent and bills and for buying food. These people seemed to be more aware of what they spent their money on and were more inclined to budget carefully, some allowing themselves a specific amount for 'going out' or socialising.

Those who smoked cigarettes or cannabis regularly reported that these substances took priority over virtually everything else. However, the cannabis smokers often had alternative methods of ensuring that their supply was constant. One such method was 'ticking'. This seemed to be particularly common amongst the younger male inter-viewees. One of the 16-year-old males described the system in detail:

A. It's like having a slate at a pub with your dealer . . . you just say, 'Well, tick me an eighth until Saturday,' because what's happening to them is they're getting someone who's a bit older picking up, say, a 'nine bar' [9 oz = quarter of a kilo] or whatever and they'll lay them on two ounces [give it to them on credit] and say, 'Look, now here's two ounces. You got two weeks. If you don't come back to me in two weeks with my money, then, you know, we'll have to sort it out some other way.' So they come to us and tick it to us for normally about a week or just under a week and then they'll collect the money a day before and then go to the dealer's the next day and pay them off. So I normally deal with a tick and I'll tick one Monday or Tuesday until about Saturday, and then, sort of, I'll just do my best to keep money aside . . . I roughly know how much I can get a day – it's normally about two pounds a day and so I know it's gonna take a little while – plus I get money from other things .

Q. Does that mean you are constantly in debt?

A. Not always, there are times where you just don't have any debts and that feels good. I've done my best to always be on time with my payment, and normally I can get someone to back me for a couple of days. Normally my girlfriend will back me . . . I say, 'Well, if you lend me a tenner now, then I'll give it you back in the next couple of days.' (MALE aged 16)

This drug distribution system made it possible for individuals to 'earn' their cannabis for free by selling small amounts to their friends without any initial outlay. As another 16-year-old male explained:

Say you get a half ounce then you can sell three-eighths and make an eighth for free . . . a half ounce is forty-five pounds and so you sell three-eighths each at fifteen and you've got one left over, so you've got it for free. (MALE aged 16)

An older female respondent also reported that she had sold small quantities of cannabis in the past:

Q. Do you always have enough money for your cannabis?

A. Well, sort of. I've sold a bit here and there when I've been totally skint, to get by. That's normally how I've done it actually.

Q. So if you're totally skint, then you'll sell a bit, but otherwise you don't?

A. It's not worth the risk really . . . I certainly wouldn't do it up here [London], but in Devon it's like perfectly acceptable that if you're a bit skint you can sell a bit of hash and no one really worries about it. (FEMALE aged 18)

Some users described a reciprocal agreement that they had with their friends, whereby the others would help them out if someone ran out of cannabis and was unable to afford any for a while:

When I have got money, if someone else wants a draw [some cannabis] and if I've already got one, I'll back them, so that it is an investment for next week. (MALE aged 16)

Use of other drugs (particularly ecstasy) seemed to be more dependent on how much money respondents had available to them at the time. In times of limited finance, they would reduce their use instead of resorting to dealing or 'ticking' for these drugs. One possible reason for this could be that, because cannabis is cheap compared to other drugs, the amounts of money involved are smaller and therefore easier to find.

6.10 Social influences: peers and friends

A traditional approach to explaining any kind of deviant or antisocial behaviour amongst young people has been to focus on the role of the social environment, with particular reference to an individual's peers. Indeed, the concept of 'peer pressure' has come to be part of popular culture: deviant behaviour is often explained away as the result of a young person 'falling in with a bad crowd'. The area of substance use is no different: a popular perception is still that young people use drugs because their friends pressurise them to do so. As we noted in the introduction, research has shown an association between peers and substance use, but the exact role that peers play and the degree of influence they exert are still unclear. Nevertheless, this concept has been the underlying paradigm for many drug education and prevention programmes which have attempted to equip young people with the skills to resist such social pressures.

Research has consistently shown that the perceived substance use involvement and related attitudes of friends are among the best indicators of this behaviour for a young person. However, as was illustrated earlier, there is a whole range of other factors involved in influencing drug and alcohol use (functions for use, expectancies, current state, gender, commitments, etc.). Nevertheless, peers are clearly important in this process, and in this study special attention was given to the discussion of peer groups and the role of friends in influencing respondents' substance-related decisions.

When asked to describe their social circle, it was not unusual for people to report that they socialised with more than one group. The size of these groups ranged from around 5 people to 40 or more. We asked each respondent to describe the drug and alcohol use of their friends and peers. Although it was common to have close friends whose substance using patterns were similar to their own, many also reported that they had friends who had quite different patterns of use. As one 18-year-old female explained:

Q. Do you use the same sort of drugs as the rest of your friends?

> A. I think so. Probably some of my friends use a lot more cannabis than I do and smoke it on a more regular basis . . . but some do less as well, so I'm sort of in the middle. I've got friends who use ecstasy and do acid as well, but I've also got friends who do nothing at all. (FEMALE aged 18)

Some of the young people differentiated between circles of friends according to their drug or alcohol use, referring to non-drug users as their 'straight friends'. These individuals often tailored their own drug use to fit into the group norms of those with whom they were socialising.

> I won't take pills [ecstasy] if I'm seeing my straight friends 'cos I don't think it's fair. (FEMALE aged 21)

Consequently, when asked what they might do with friends on a special occasion, the answer was often dependent on which group of friends was celebrating.

'Peer pressure'

This concept was often spontaneously mentioned by interviewees without prompting. Although this observation supports suggestions that this idea has become part of popular culture, the phrase was generally mentioned because people disagreed with the concept. The general opinion seemed to be that substance use was engaged in through personal choice rather than as a result of social pressures. As an 18-year-old female explained:

> A couple of friends have said, 'You know we're getting some Es, would you like some?' but there's been no pressure or anything. It's just been just asking. (FEMALE aged 18)

Only one participant reported that they had felt pressurised into using drugs. However, it should be noted that this particular individual differed from the majority of the sample, as he strongly disapproved of most drug use. This seemed to be the result of him experiencing problems with heavy cannabis and LSD use. Unlike the others, who tended to describe current use and experiences in the interview, he was trying to explain in retrospect how things had gone wrong for him. The only other respondent to recognise the force of 'peer pressure' described how friends had pressurised her to *stop* using drugs:

> People are so against them (temazepam) that I wouldn't really dare tell anyone that I'd ever done them really . . . my friends were like, 'Give them up . . . [[. . . . . .]] hell, just give them up, they're no good for you,' and so I suppose gradually through all this – you know, the peer pressure thing – then I did. (FEMALE aged 18)

The data suggest that friends are definitely associated with the opportunity to use drugs, but there was little to support the notion of 'peer pressure'. After all, it is not uncommon for an individual to be motivated to share with friends an activity that they enjoy, for example, encouraging a friend to try climbing or scuba diving.

Some research has suggested that young people choose to make friends with people who share their own values and behaviours or that people who are friends tend to become more alike in these dimensions (Kandel 1985). Whilst this might hold for very close friends or 'best friends', the data presented here suggest that attitudes and values towards substance use does not necessarily promote or preclude friendships (or at least inclusion in certain social networks). Instead, young people may socialise with individuals who exhibit a range of behaviours, values and attitudes. It is therefore probably most helpful to use the phrase 'peer influence' rather than 'peer pressure' or 'peer preference', as peers clearly do play a role in influencing drug-related decisions. Rather than being passive in social situations, and therefore subject to pressure, this group of young people described a process in which they weighed up a complex range of pros and cons and formulated their own attitudes, values and behaviours. They recognised the influence that their friends had over them, but, although acknowledging this, reported that they made their own decisions. Of course, an individual who wants to try a substance is probably much more likely to do so if they know someone with a similar inclination. Similarly, somebody who habitually uses a drug with a particular group of people who then finds that the rest of the group no longer want to pursue this activity may be influenced to cut down or stop their use. The following quote is from a 20-year-old male who described how he stopped his heavy use of ecstasy:

A. At one stage . . . we used to go out from Friday to Monday and I used to do about four or five in each club and then during the week when you're coming down it can really murder you . . . I lost a lot of weight as well – you don't eat . . . then after a while the people that I used to do it with, a couple of them got jobs and then we stopped going out . . . the people that I started going round with, they never done nothing, so 'cos they never done nothing, I didn't want to stand there and do it on my own, so I stopped.

Q. But you could have found other people if you'd wanted to carry on?

A. Yeah, it's not to do with the people I hang around with, it's more to do with me. I just wanted to stop because I lost so much weight.

To go out and specially find a peer so that they can have some company for this type of social activity did not seem to be a rational choice for these young people. Nor did exerting overt pressure on their current friends, as this meant risking exclusion from the group. For example, the following excerpt is from an interview with a 16-year-old female. She reported that she had had the opportunity to try various drugs, including amphetamines and ecstasy, but has so far chosen not to. However, if she decided otherwise, she knows people with whom she might try:

Q. Do you think that your friends' drug use has affected what drugs you use or don't use?

A. Probably does affect you a bit, but I'm not pressurised or anything. If I don't want to do it, they're not going to pressurise me into doing it. Like, sometimes if other people are doing it and I don't want to, they don't say, 'Go on,' because we're not like that. (FEMALE aged 16)

Another young woman also recognised the influence that her peers might have on her:

I think if I was to be friends with people who do take acid and ecstasy . . . and more speed, then I think that I would probably be a bit more inclined . . . I mean, if they were taking it more and they were still here – not dead – then I'd probably think, 'Yeah, it's not that bad,' but because I don't really know many people who do, then I don't really hear that much about experiences, and even when I do, it doesn't really turn me on that much, and I'm not thinking, 'Wow, I've got to go and do it.' (FEMALE aged 19)

First use and the influence of friends

There were some reports that close friends or 'best friends' had played an important role when they were first initiated into the use of a particular drug. It was quite common for individuals to share the experience of initiation with a friend for 'moral support'. There were sometimes reports that on subsequent occasions the same friends would want to accompany each other for the initiation into other types of substance use:

My best friend at home, we did all our first drugs together, like first got stoned, first did an E. (FEMALE aged 18)

Another female described how she first used amphetamines and ecstasy with her best friend, and that they always made sure that they were by themselves. This rule that they had made for themselves had led to them refusing the opportunity to use other drugs:

Q. Have you ever used cocaine?

> A. I have had the opportunity lots of times . . . it's just that . . . well, the same situation as doing ecstasy. I always do things with my friend [for the first time] and we'd always do them alone, rather than doing them around a group of friends, so that they couldn't freak us out or whatever . . . so we'd be in our own little world. (FEMALE aged 21)

Others did not necessarily have a particular friend that they liked to be with when trying a drug for the first time, but mentioned that the people they were with would still be an important factor. An ideal situation would be with a small group of close friends, as the following quote from a 20-year-old male talking about how he might try heroin once or twice illustrates:

> It would have to be with a good circle of friends if I was trying it for the first time . . . I like to be with people I trust when I try any drug for the first time, and with people who are also trying it for the first time . . . so that you can talk about what's happening . . . and also with someone who knows what they are doing. (MALE aged 20)

Similar feelings were expressed by another respondent:

> I don't like to do things on my own . . . I like to have at least one person on my wavelength, otherwise I might get paranoid . . . if I go out with someone it's normally a close friend. I want to go out with someone who I trust in case something does go wrong . . . you know, if I had a bad reaction to anything . . . so it always has to be someone who I trust completely and who would know what to do if something does happen . . . and the person that I go out with I won't leave . . . I'll stay with them all night. (FEMALE aged 19)

Patterns of use

Friends or peers were reported to influence some people to use less of a drug or less frequently. For example, a 20-year-old male described how his decisions to use ecstasy were often affected by his girlfriend's decision to use the drug:

Q. When you go to clubs with your girlfriend, does she usually have something?

> A. Not very often, but she will every now and again.

Q. Does that affect whether you do anything?

> A. No . . . well, it might in that sometimes if she's not, then I'll make a decision. I'll think, 'No, I'm not, 'cos I don't want her to feel left out.' (MALE aged 20)

Others described how the influence of their friends often led to them using more of a drug than they had meant to. For more details of the data on this issue see Chapter 8, 'Deciding on limits for substance use'.

6.11 Media influences

Of all the types of substance use discussed in the interviews, the influence of media coverage was almost exclusively mentioned in relation to ecstasy use. Some of the interviewees appeared to have been very influenced by the news stories of ecstasy-related deaths. In some cases, this had resulted in the conclusion that the possible benefits of using this drug were not worth the attendant risks. In contrast, the lack of high-profile media stories relating to amphetamine use seemed to have resulted in the deduction that this was far less dangerous than ecstasy. The following excerpts illustrate this in more detail:

> I didn't try ecstasy, I tried speed [amphetamines] first, because, I don't know why, but I thought that speed was . . . I suppose it's the media really, 'cos they don't really hook on to speed so much, so I thought, 'Oh, I'll try some speed first.' (FEMALE age 21)

Q. Why wouldn't you take pills [ecstasy]?

> A. A couple of people I know have done 'em, but I think people are scared to do 'em, 'cos you see people in the newspapers and that, people dying . . . so people are scared of it. (MALE age 16)

Q. You say it's very unlikely that you'll try ecstasy, speed or LSD in the next year. What do you think is your main reason for not wanting to try them?

> A. I'm scared of what the consequences might be . . . like on the news you see that this guy he took ecstasy for his first time and he died, and I think that if I do that then that could happen to me. So it's not worth taking the chance. (MALE age 17)

However, the influence that media reports about ecstasy had had on other respondents seemed to be minimal. In some cases, they had either dismissed the accounts completely or offered explanations which cast the victims as incompetent drug users. In addition to this, some users had constructed specific rules for themselves which they believed would keep them safe. One example of this was given by a 20-year-old male:

> People are weird about the dangers of it [ecstasy] 'cos of all the hype you get in the media . . . but that really is dogma. If you use ecstasy, you find out that it really isn't as dangerous as they say in the media, and the dangers can be reduced by watching your temperature, drinking – not drinking too much, the right amount – and by taking salt and isotonic drinks and avoiding hot and cramped conditions like you get in clubs. (MALE age 20)

7 TRANSITIONS

So far, our analysis has focused on the general factors which were reported as being influential in the day-to-day substance-related decisions made by the sample. However, from a health perspective, initiation or intermittent drug use does not necessarily carry the greatest risks. Instead, the transition to regular or excessive use is likely to increase the health risks substantially. The initial stages of substance use are clearly relevant to this process, as they form an intrinsic part of the path followed to habitual or problematic substance use. However, this path is by no means inevitable. It is likely that the majority of young people who use drugs and alcohol on a 'recreational' basis are unlikely to experience significant health problems as a result of their use. Nevertheless, if the factors that contribute to potentially problematic use can be identified, better interventions aiming to avoid this transition can be developed.

Any discussion of this type is fraught with problems. What constitutes regular use of one drug could be classed as intermittent use of another. Amongst this sample, it seems that there were very different patterns of use for different substances. For example, the majority of people who had used cigarettes, alcohol or cannabis in the three months prior to interview had done so more than once a week, whereas use was generally less frequent for the other drugs which are perceived to have longer-acting effects.

One person's definition of regular use may substantially differ from that of another. However, owing to the qualitative nature of this study we were able to work with a loose definition of this term. Respondents who reported using a drug on more than an intermittent experimental basis, or who defined themselves as a 'current user' of the substance, were asked to describe what they thought had most influenced changes in their patterns of use (transitions). This included both escalations in their consumption and (where relevant) factors associated with the reductions in use. If an individual was unable to describe their use of a substance in terms of typical use or patterns of use then it was taken to be still in experimental stages.

The set of factors which emerged from the data closely resemble those identified earlier in the report as influencing decisions concerning which substances to use. The remainder of this chapter is organised into similar categories to those of Chapter 6. Each of the factors is illustrated with examples pertaining to specific drug types. Data are not available on all substances as the number of people in the sample who reported regular use of the different drug types was small.

7.1 Functions

A few respondents reported that the discovery that amphetamines helped them to work more efficiently or helped to relieve tiredness had been the main influence that led to them using the drug regularly, as the following excerpt illustrates:

Q. So did it start off that you used it mainly in the evenings?

A. Yeah . . . if I was feeling a bit tired, if I had been working on a building site from six a.m., then by six in the evening you're just knackered, you know . . . you go down the pub and it gets to the point where you're going home at ten o'clock and all your mates are going on. So . . . I'd dab a bit of speed and it was just literally a pick-me-up, and that was it. And then it ended up being pretty substantial. (MALE aged 20)

This particular young man had gradually increased his use of amphetamines to the point where he used several times a day for a period of six months.

A 21-year-old female was using amphetamines daily at the time of interview. She was among others who found that this drug helped them to be more sociable:

I used to go out and people were telling me in clubs how good it was and someone would say, 'Do you want any speed? If you're feeling [[bad]] then do some of this' . . . and I did feel happy when I was taking it, and the first time I took it I had the best night ever . . . I started having a really good time, and I started realising that people were talking to me and I started hearing people saying, 'Oh, that [name], she's really good fun,' and that would mean a lot to me, and I started respecting myself a bit more. (FEMALE aged 21)

Deciding that a particular substance was better than another at fulfilling certain functions could lead to increased use of one drug and a corresponding decrease in the use of another. For example, a 19-year-old female that we interviewed had recently stopped using large quantities of ecstasy and amphetamines and had started using more alcohol with her friends. This change in patterns of use was prompted when she began to realise that the feelings of depression that she was experiencing during the week could be related to her stimulant use at weekends. She subsequently reduced her ecstasy use but reported that she still felt that she needed something to facilitate social interactions. She found that drinking alcohol helped to do this without her feeling depressed afterwards.

7. 2 Current physical or psychological state

A common factor reported to have influenced a reduction in the use of some substances was concerns about health. These included both physical and mental health concerns. One example was depression: some young people reported that they started using amphetamines or one of the opiates regularly, as they found that it relieved feelings of depression. In contrast to this, one respondent stopped using ecstasy and amphetamines at weekends when she realised that it was making her feel depressed during the week:

A. During the week after I've taken it, I just feel completely depressed . . . it doesn't matter what you do – you can do things that would make you perfectly happy at any other time – you just feel utterly depressed the whole time, and nothing I could do would make me feel better.

Q. So to start with did you get depression afterwards?

A. Not really. If I did . . . I just didn't recognise it . . . I'd just think it was normal, because I think everyone gets a bit down, so I wouldn't have recognised it, I suppose, until it got to the point where it was so much that it had to be the drugs.

Q. When do you think you recognised that?

A. About six months ago, and then I stopped taking it soon afterwards 'cos I just couldn't stand it . . . during that depression all you want is more ecstasy, 'cos you feel that that's the only thing that can make you happy again or put you on that high that you get on it. (FEMALE aged 19)

7.3 Expectancies

Increased use was often associated with an individual liking the effects of a drug and therefore expecting positive effects from repeated use. In contrast to this, several respondents also described how positive expectancies about a substance had gradually become more negative and led to a reduction in use. This was particularly common amongst participants who had significantly reduced their alcohol use:

I got out of it [stopped drinking] gradually really, but I just hate the feeling of being pissed. I hate that head spinning sort of thing, the falling round the place, the being sick, feeling sick. I don't like it at all, you just seem to lose it. I mean at least when you do a pill [ecstasy] you're still together enough to sit down and have a conversation with someone and maybe even blag [convince] someone that you're straight! Whereas when you're pissed there's just no chance, you're just a mess, aren't you ? (FEMALE aged 18)

Others explained how they had decided that the pleasurable effects from using a drug were not worth suffering the after-effects, as the following quote illustrates:

A. I want to try and cut down on my speed 'cos I feel groggy for the next two or three days after.

Q. Groggy? Do you mean grumpy or depressed or . . .?

A. Depressed. It's more like a mild hangover for about three days. (MALE aged 21)

7.4 Commitments/changing priorities

Factors concerning commitments or changing priorities tended to be associated with a reduction in the use of a substance rather than an escalation. Examples of this included starting college, playing sport or wanting to join the army:

A. I'm playing for a football team every Wednesday night and I do wanna carry on playing football, and so I do wanna cut down on cigarettes and puff [cannabis].

Q. Why would it stop you playing football?

A. Because it makes you unfit. About twenty mins into a game I start coughing, and I'm always spitting. It blocks up my throat a lot. (MALE aged 16)

7.5 Social influences

As discussed in Section 6.10 on social influences, the data from this study provided little evidence for overt pressure being exerted by peer groups. Respondents recognised that their peers had some influence over their behaviour, but maintained that their substance use was their own choice. The only person to give any account of experiencing pressure was trying to explain in retrospect why his use had become so heavy. Even in this case, he did not report overt pressure, rather that his perceptions of the underlying opinions of his peers had influenced his behaviour. A few accounts suggested that peers played a larger role in influencing use of a substance to escalate. For example, one 16-year-old female explained how she had first used cannabis when she was about 13 whilst at a friend's house, but had not started to use it regularly until she began mixing with a group of boys who were regular cannabis users. Another female of the same age had had a similar experience:

A. I tried it [cannabis] once then I didn't try it again until I started hanging round with a new group of people . . . I moved schools when I was nearly fifteen and it was a bigger group of us and they were more into that. That's when I started to use it more.

Q. Do you think they influenced you to start using it?

A. Maybe at first, but you'd have to have bought it yourself afterwards so they didn't pressurise me. (FEMALE aged 16)

On the other hand, there were also reports that friends had also influenced a reduction in the use of a drug. For example, an 18-year-old female reported she had reduced her use of amphetamines in the hope that by stopping her use she could influence her friend to stop too.

A. My friend was doing it [taking speed daily] at the same time. She did it to lose weight and she got so skinny 'cos she just wouldn't eat. You don't get hungry on speed. She was getting really ill off that, it was really starting to affect her physically. She was just a bag of bones really, and then we had this massive argument one day and that was it, I stopped after that.

Q. So you stopped immediately after the argument?

A. I stopped because I didn't want to see her getting more like that, and then gradually she stopped . . . because I think I'd made her realise what was going on. (FEMALE aged 18)

Another female respondent explained how all her drug use experience had been with the same best friend. Now that this friend was thinking of having children and was intending to stop going to nightclubs and using stimulants, she thought that this would result in her stopping these activities too.

Several girls mentioned that they thought that their boyfriends had been particularly influential over their drug use, both in escalating and cutting down use. However, male respondents who mentioned girlfriends as influential only associated them with a reduction in their substance use.

7.6 Availability/finance

In some cases, when an individual had decided that they wanted to reduce or stop their use of a substance, they deliberately made it difficult for themselves to obtain more of it. For example, one 19-year-old female used to live with someone who was dealing amphetamines, but moved when she decided to stop using:

> A. For about a year and a half I was constantly taking it . . . not every single day, but the majority of days, because I didn't have to pay for it and it was there on a plate for me . . . and then I didn't take it for ages, nearly a year.

Q. Was that deliberate?

> A. Yeah. I moved out and I wanted to get myself back on track because I'd gone a bit downhill. I didn't have a job and just basically bummed around. (FEMALE aged 19)

A 20-year-old male interviewee reported that he had decreased his use for financial reasons. He had decided that he wanted to spend his limited money on other things:

> I've decided that I'm going to try to stop taking all drugs. Well, the only drug that I'll still do . . . that I like doing, is cocaine, but I can't really do that on a regular basis because it's too expensive, . . . I'd love to do that. . . . about a month ago, two months ago, I was doing that . . . regular every other day sort of thing, but then I got into a bit of debt, so I had to stop that as well till I'd paid that off. I paid that off and after that I said to myself I can't afford to buy it. Once in a blue moon, yeah, but not every other day, it's too expensive. (MALE aged 20)

7.7 Environment

A temporary change in environment, such as going on holiday, seemed to be associated with an escalation in substance use for some people, which was then maintained once back home.

Q. Can you describe how your use of speed has changed since you first used it?

> A. When I first used it [aged fifteen] I took it and then didn't take it again for about another three or four months . . . but it was never a regular thing until after my A levels finished . . . I went to Ibiza and Tenerife and I took it regularly for a whole summer. I took it practically every night when I was on holiday, and then I came back and it's sort of been a regular thing every time I arrange to go clubbing. (FEMALE aged 20)

> A. I went to Spain to stay with this friend, and her mum used to let us stay out all night till six o'clock in the morning. Because we're a lot bigger than the Spanish girls, we could get served anywhere. We were going out and getting really drunk. When I came back from there I smoked a lot more as well. (FEMALE aged 16)

Other types of environmental change were also associated with changes in substance use patterns. These were generally changes that affected a respondent's peer group, such as starting a new school or college.

8 DECIDING ON LIMITS FOR SUBSTANCE USE

We have established that decisions about drug and alcohol use are multi-faceted. The principal focus of this study was on how young people decide whether or not to use a specific substance on a particular occasion. However, there are other decisions to be made which concern substance use (see p. 9): for example, an individual must decide how much of a given substance they are going to use (size of doses) and whether to set themselves definite limits within a certain time period. The data collected from the quantitative questionnaire show that the reported amounts of a substance used on a 'typical using day' differed significantly from individual to individual. For example, the average number of cannabis cigarettes that respondents smoked on a typical day was five. However, the range was between 1 and 25. Similarly, the average for ecstasy was 1.75 tablets and the range was 0.5–6 tablets.

Combining this data with that collected from the qualitative interview, it appeared that the intensity of use was not dictated purely by availability, finance or some other external circumstance. Instead, many respondents had conscious ways of limiting their substance use.

When asked how they limited their consumption, responses divided most people into one of two categories: those who limited their intake by dose (amount) for fear of ill-effects and those who continued to use until time or money dictated otherwise. Using time or money to limit use was a deliberate strategy for some, though for others it seemed to be by default rather than through a conscious decision. The data also suggest that an individual who uses 'dose limiting' strategies for one drug might use a different strategy to limit use of another. For example, in the following excerpt a 21-year-old female described how she limits her use of ecstasy and amphetamines in different ways:

Q. How do you decide how many [ecstasy tablets] you're going to have?

    A. I always get two just in case they're rubbish, and so then I'll take two, but I usually end up with one left over.

Q. So if it's a good pill you won't just take the other one just because it's there?

    A. No, not unless I'm out with [name], who will make me take it . . . well, not make me, but she'll say, 'Don't you want the other one,' several times over and then I will take it.

Q. Do you regret it afterwards or not?

    A. Well, yeah, because I never get any higher. I just stay the same as I am, and so in a way it's a waste as I could have taken it the next week.

Q. Do you have a similar thing with speed?

    A. No, with speed I'll use the whole lot. If I go out with three grams then I'll use three grams.

Q. So do you limit the amount you take with you?

    A. Yeah, I'll only take a certain amount. I would normally carry two pills and two grams of speed, and my friend would do the same. But if one of us wasn't high enough, then we would give each other what we've got. (FEMALE aged 21)

A male respondent described how, although he and his friends were fairly heavy users of ecstasy, they still set themselves clear limits.

A. If we're going to use ecstasy, then we have a set amount . . . we only acquire that amount, because of the likelihood of you on your comedown thinking, 'Oh, I'll just have another to bring me back up' . . . and that's when you can start to encounter problems

Q. So what are your limits?

A. Two or three pills depending on how strong they are. (MALE aged 20)

Others reported that they had calculated suitable limits for their drug consumption to avoid unwanted side-effects. As a 19-year-old female explained:

Q. Do you set yourself any limits with amphetamines?

A. I wouldn't take a whole gram. At the most I would take a half . . . I just don't like that whole feeling of not being able to sleep.

Q. What about cannabis?

A. The problem with smoking is that I can't discipline myself to like ration it out. It's more like if I've got it then I'll smoke it, and when that runs out, if I've got no money, then I'll just have to have a break. (FEMALE aged 19)

Limiting the quantity used is perhaps more of an issue in the case of alcohol, as it is much more widely available than illicit drugs. In general, people who used drugs at nightclubs took what they were going to use with them into the club, as they were reluctant to purchase from unknown sources. Consequently, decisions over amounts to use were made well in advance of consumption. However, when describing how alcohol consumption was limited, respondents showed more concern about avoiding negative effects from this drug. Current physical and psychological state also seemed to influence decisions concerning how use was limited. Respondents reported that they took into account such factors as how much they had eaten and how strongly they were experiencing the effects from alcoholic drinks already consumed. In general, participants seemed to have learned roughly how much they could drink before risking negative effects from alcohol, though some were still uncertain if mixing it with other substances. The following quotes illustrate this further:

Q. How do you tell where your limit is? Is it when you've reached a certain feeling or do you count how many drinks you've had?

A. When I reach a certain feeling, when my head starts spinning . . . but usually I stop before that. It's only very occasionally I get to that point. Usually I just drink enough to get me quite 'tipsy'. (FEMALE aged 16)

A. Last year, when I didn't know where to stop and I just went over the top a lot, I got ill quite a lot. Now I know where my limit is. I don't drink as much and I don't get ill.

Q. How can you tell where your limit is? Is it how you feel? Or do you think, 'Well, I've had three beers . . .'?

> A. Yeah, I usually think, 'Well I've had that much' . . . I haven't eaten much, if I have much more I'm gonna be ill. Depends on what you've eaten during the day as well . . . If you've eaten a lot you can usually take more . . .

Q. What if you're smoking cannabis? Does that make any difference?

> A. Yes, it does. You usually drink less when you're smoking it, 'cos it can make you ill as well. If you mix the two it makes you feel a bit funny. (FEMALE aged 16)

Q. Do you have a limit that you set yourself when you are drinking?

> A. Yeah. I like being 'happy drunk'. I don't like getting to the stage where I can see what's happening in front of me and I can't control it . . . I know where my limit is, and I know if I drink any more when I think, 'Ok, you've had enough now,' then I'm gonna end up like that. (FEMALE aged 19)

Similar strategies were described in association with other drugs, such as amphetamines:

> A [Talking about using amphetamines.] I've always been very careful. I'm not greedy, you know. If I'm going to go out, I want to reach a certain point, then that's me happy . . .

Q. So do you set yourself a limit in terms of quantities of drug, or do you wait for a certain effect and that's your limit?

> A. Usually in quantities of drug, because I tend not to be able to afford any more. But there's no need to completely lose it . . . you know, if you're gonna get stoned, then there's no point getting so pointlessly and stupidly stoned that you can't enjoy the fact that you're stoned with your friends . . .

Q. So what sort of limits do you set yourself?

> A. Well, it usually works out that I can only afford one pill anyway or a little bit of speed . . . I don't really feel the need to go out and do eight . . . even if I had the money, I don't think I'd do it. I'd still only go out and do one. (MALE aged 21)

8.1 Finances

For some respondents, the amount of money that they took with them on a night out was the major factor that determined how much of a chosen substance they used. While this was a conscious decision for some, for others it seemed to be more a force of circumstance. The following quotes illustrate these contrasting views:

Q. Do you set yourself any limits when you go out?

> A. To a certain extent. Not because I actually intend to but because I only take enough money with me to get, say, one pill, two pills or whatever.

Q. Is that a deliberate thing?

> A. Yeah, I suppose so, because I'll have to budget it out anyway, and so I'll say, 'Right, I've got thirty pounds for this evening,' and then I'll put that in my wallet and I won't take any of my cards out with me, I'll just take my money. (FEMALE aged 18)

A. I think some people just know their limit and they don't really want to get ill, and so they stick to that . . . whereas people like me don't really care and so just keep going . . . I think that they get to a point and think, 'No, if I do any more it won't be enjoyable.'

Q. Whereas you keep going?

A. Yeah.

Q. So if you go out drinking, what dictates when you stop?

A. Either money or time.

Q. Do you deliberately take a certain amount of money when you go out drinking?

A. No, it's just what I can afford. (FEMALE aged 20)

A. We just spend all our money until it's gone or until you can't get any more . . . If we can't get any more drugs then we'll spend the rest on drink. (FEMALE aged 18)

However, for drugs such as cannabis that are generally bought in amounts that are large enough for repeated doses, money was not reported to play such an important role. Instead the effects themselves were usually the limiting factors.

Q. If you're smoking with friends, do you have a certain limit when you stop?

A. Sometimes I do and sometimes I do keep going.

Q. How do you decide?

A. It's just the way I feel, like if I feel I don't want no more . . . the way cannabis makes me feel is sort of lazy and drowsy and my eyes sort of feel heavy, and when I know that I'm getting to that sort of stage, I don't smoke no more unless I'm in my home. If I know I'm not – I'm at my friends' house and I've got to go home from there then I'll say 'I've got to go'. (FEMALE aged 16)

8.2 Time

Time appeared to be more important for those drinking in public establishments (because the licensing laws limited availability) or those using stimulants (some users wanted to sleep at a certain time). However, this was by no means universal, as many of the stimulant users did not indicate that time played any part in their decision-making. Instead, it tended to be that those who reported limiting their intake according to the time of day or night had work commitments and therefore wanted to ensure that they got a reasonable amount of sleep. The following excerpts further illustrate this relation-ship between time and substance use.

A. If it was something like an eighteenth or a twenty-first [birthday party] or something, then we'd start at like about eight o'clock. And if we knew we was going to go all the way through to like six in the morning at a club then we'd probably take speed like eight hours before, because we knew like by the time the eight hours are up when we leave the club we're going to like come down by the time we get home . . . [and] be OK to sleep, so it's probably like eight hours.

Q. So you think about the time span?

A. Yeah, we always think about the time span. We don't like think, 'Oh, we've got two hours left in a club, well, let's pop an E,' or, . . . take some speed, 'cos we know that we'll still be high when we get home, and you wanna go to sleep and you just can't . . . You'll end up just [[messing]] up that day as well. (MALE aged 18)

Q. How do you pace yourself?

A. If I've just got one wrap, then I take the whole lot, but most of the time I've got two wraps . . . Say the night is from ten till four or six, then I'll have one at about eleven and then one at about half one or two just to keep me going.

Q. So is there a certain time after which you won't have any more?

A. The only time I wouldn't is . . . say if the night was ending at four, then I wouldn't take it at three o'clock because I've only got an hour left . . . that would probably be pointless. (FEMALE aged 20)

A. Say I've got to get up at nine o'clock in the morning. I'll have a smoke [cannabis] till two . . . I'll set a bit of a limit. I'll say, 'Well, I'll go home at two 'cos then I can have some food and that' . . . I'm a bit pushy about my sleep as well. I have to have at least six hours 'cos otherwise it just runs me down. I don't like it . . . I used to just come in and then go whenever I want, but then at the end of the week I'd just crash and I couldn't handle that, it's just annoying. (MALE aged 16)

Another factor identified as influencing consumption limits was concurrent substance use. For example, some respondents reported that they rarely drank alcohol when using ecstasy or amphetamines, whilst others drank very little compared with their normal rates of consumption. This decision tended to be attributed to the beliefs that alcohol reduced the effects of these stimulants or had dehydrating properties which could increase negative effects.

With those drugs perceived to have longer-acting effects, such as LSD, users tended to talk more of limiting the frequency of use rather than the amount consumed on a single occasion. Unlike the other substances discussed, one dose of LSD can trigger effects that last up to 12 hours, and so repeated administration is unnecessary. Respondents suggested that the risks associated with 'overdoing it' were avoidable if drugs such as ecstasy and LSD were used with 'respect' and in moderation. However, 'moderation' appeared to mean very different things to different respondents, from only 'once or twice a week – at weekends' (MALE aged 20) to monthly or less frequently.

SUMMARY AND RECOMMENDATIONS

This concluding section summarises the key results from the study and explores practical implications and recommendations for education, prevention and research activities. The study was designed as a preliminary exploration of how young people decide whether or not to use drugs or alcohol and the range of factors that influence these decisions. Our conclusions are, of course, tentative and require replication and further study. Nevertheless, we hope that these findings will contribute to the development of education and prevention initiatives by suggesting new areas that offer potential for intervention strategies. In framing the results summary, we again stress that the 50 young people interviewed were not randomly recruited nor meant to represent the greater population of this age group in the UK. Instead, the purposive sample and the methods chosen were specifically designed to provide insight into the range of processes and factors involved in drug and alcohol-related decision-making.

Analysis of the data yielded 11 factors which influenced decision-making for this sample. We categorise these as 'individual factors' (functions for substance use, expectancies, current state, gender influences, commitments and boundaries) and 'social/contextual factors' (environment, availability, finance, social influences and media influences) (see schematic diagram on p. 67). A focus on any one of these factors could provide an opportunity for prevention measures to influence the decisions made by young people (see Boys *et al.* in press b). Moreover, addressing several of these factors at once, could strengthen the effectiveness of such prevention programmes considerably by tackling the issue from several stances. However, in view of the exploratory, qualitative nature of the study, caution must be exercised in ascribing weights to the relative importance of different influences. Whilst our set of decision-making influences is unlikely to be complete and further work in this area is necessary, it does provide a good starting point for a relatively under-researched area.

Recommendation 1

Substance use prevention initiatives aimed at young people may be more effective if they address several decision-making factors concurrently, rather than focusing on one particular issue.

9.1 Social context of substance use

Our participants generally associated substance use with socialising with their friends, and as enhancing social activities. Taking a substance whilst alone was uncommon. Most people reported use of alcohol, cannabis or one of the 'dance drugs' when in the company of their friends. Opiate and benzodiazepine use was rare, was more likely to

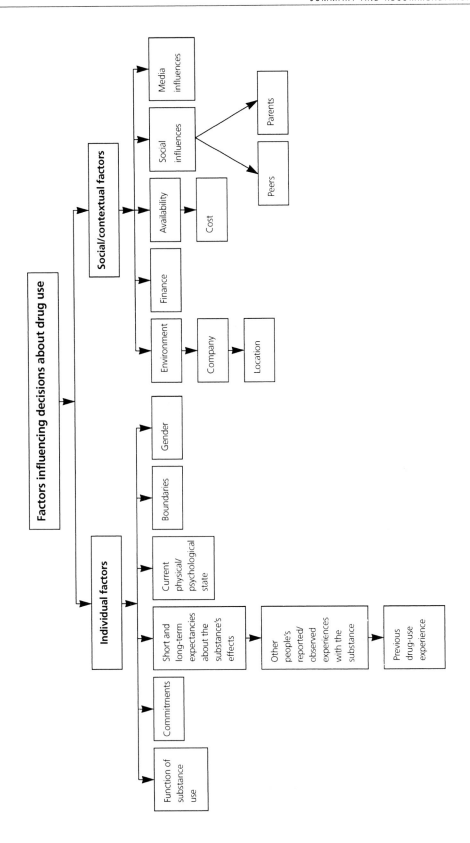

Figure 9.1 Factors influencing drug- and alcohol-related decisions

be described as a means of coping with negative moods and events and was associated with respondents who were experiencing social problems, such as homelessness. American research has identified a range of predisposing factors among young people which are associated with the development of chronic substance use problems. These include having parents or siblings with drug problems, family disruption, poor educational achievement, truancy and exclusion from school and social deprivation (see Lloyd [1998] for a review). It is important to remember that the sample interviewed for this study was not selected to reflect young people particularly vulnerable to developing future drug problems, although they were not excluded. It is likely that the factors that influence decision-making processes among vulnerable groups will be similar to those identified in this study. If this is so, exploring the functions that drug use serves for this group may be useful in informing the development of targeted drug prevention initiatives.

9.2 Gender issues

There were almost no differences between males and females and their peers with respect to the decision-making focus of the study. The only consistently reported difference reflected the quantities of substances consumed and preferred types. Overall, males and male peers were observed to drink more alcohol than females and smoke more cannabis. However, amongst 16- and 17-year-olds, females were considered to drink more heavily than the males, who preferred to smoke cannabis instead. Gender differences in substance preference were also observed amongst the older respondents. Males and females were described as looking for different types of effects from drugs, with females preferring physical effects, such as an increase in energy, and males the hallucinogenic or perceptual distortion effects produced by drugs such as LSD. These preferences were supported by the data. Many of the female respondents preferred amphetamines and were often very wary of LSD; in contrast, males often reported the opposite preference. In this study we did not collect detailed information about the role of substance use in adolescent courtship. However, anecdotal evidence from respondents suggests that this may be an important area to investigate.

9.3 Commitments

Some of the young people we interviewed reported that they took their role obligations and commitments into consideration when making decisions about substance use. The extent to which this factor influenced drug and alcohol-related choices differed throughout the sample. Overall respondents seemed to be less likely to use long-acting drugs such as LSD, amphetamines and ecstasy if they had a commitment to fulfil (e.g. attend college; go to paid work). Cannabis and alcohol were still used by many during the previous day, but often in smaller quantities. There were also reports that users often took into account how they expected to feel after taking certain drugs when deciding what (if anything) to consume. If the user had to get up early the following morning they would probably choose to use a substance that they did not expect to feel negative after-effects from. One example of this was using cocaine or ecstasy instead of amphetamines. This suggests that young people may use problem-avoiding strategies that influence their drug consumption choices. Again this may represent a fruitful area for developing prevention and harm reduction responses. In addition, it was not always clear that young people associated problems they were experiencing in different areas of their life with their substance use.

Recommendation 2

Conducting individual audits which make the connection between problem behaviours and drug consumption might prove valuable in encouraging behavioural changes.

9.4 Boundaries

Respondents with similar drug-related experience tended to share the same basic boundaries governing the types of drug use they regarded as acceptable or unacceptable. We found overwhelmingly negative attitudes towards crack, heroin and all forms of injecting drug use amongst the sample. Even the few who admitted to using these drugs reported that their peers generally opposed such behaviour. This suggests that these forms of drug use, often associated with the most serious and long-standing problems, are still marginalised even amongst groups of fairly heavy recreational users. For some, cocaine powder was also grouped alongside these, whereas other, more experienced drug users saw cocaine as similar to ecstasy and amphetamines. More recent research has indicated that perceptions of cocaine may be shifting further (Boys et al. 1999). Alcohol, cannabis and tobacco had been used by the majority of the sample, and again seemed to be perceived as distinct from (and less dangerous than) other types of substance use.

Recommendation 3

Intervention strategies that aim to strengthen existing behavioural boundaries may inhibit transitions to more harmful patterns of substance use.

9.5 Functions for substance use

Perhaps the most striking finding is that, at an individual level, a major influence on drug and alcohol-related decisions seems to be the specific function that the individual is seeking to fulfil by using a psychoactive substance. This not only impacts on whether that person decides to use a substance or not, it also affects the *type* of substance chosen and the *amount* (dose) consumed. The functions described by the present sample ranged from facilitating activity of one sort or another (such as work or dancing for long periods) to changing mood or helping to manage the effects from other drugs (such as using cannabis to help ease the 'comedown' as the effects of a stimulant wore off). The following list summarises the functions most commonly described in the data. Drugs or alcohol were used to

- increase energy;
- relax;
- dance;
- get away from problems;
- help manage effects from other drugs;
- decrease inhibitions;
- relieve boredom;
- relieve depressive thoughts;
- suppress appetite /diet;
- increase motivation to get things done;
- facilitate work;
- increase confidence.

Different substances served different types of function, and respondents often mentioned several substances that they used to fulfil a variety of needs. For example, a typical profile of a relatively experienced user might be that they use alcohol when socialising in public with friends, as it helps them to relax and feel more confident; ecstasy or amphetamines when going to a nightclub and wanting to stay up all night dancing and feeling energetic; and cannabis to manage the effects of the 'comedown' from stimulants (to relax at home with friends or to induce sleep). The list of different functions is likely to grow as more work is conducted in this area. It is hoped that this will provide the impetus for further research that looks specifically at this theme.

Recommendation 4
Further research is needed to identify the range of functions that substance use serves for young people. Functions are likely to vary by both the drug type and the context of use.

A functional perspective may also prove valuable in the development of more effective education programmes. In addition to identifying different contexts of use (such as use of amphetamines to facilitate work) there is an opportunity to develop strategies which encourage recognition of the functions that substance use plays for some young people and which promote alternative means for fulfilling these roles (see Boys *et al.* in press a). In essence, this is a contemporary twist to the familiar diversion emphasis present in many prevention programmes. Rather than assuming that substance use stems from boredom our suggestion is that programmes should acknowledge that substance use is taking place as a dynamic behaviour in order to meet specific functions. It would be highly optimistic to expect that the desire to take psychoactive substances will be extinguished by diverting young people's attention towards exciting alternative leisure pursuits. However, subtle effects may occur, and these may be sufficient to alter the balance in decision-making over the longer term. We conclude that a functional approach holds promise for a more finely differentiated perspective for educators.

Recommendation 5

Educational programmes should develop and evaluate a functional perspective on drug use. Young people should be encouraged to consider the functions that drug or alcohol use has for users and seek alternative methods of fulfilling these functions. Diversionary programmes should be modified to target the specific functions that substance use serves for young people.

9.6 Expectancies

The second major influence identified concerned an individual's expectancies about the effects of a substance. In support of the alcohol expectancy research (e.g. Christiansen *et al.* 1989), our data suggest that expectancies concerning use of the other substances studied could have similar links with consumption patterns, although rigorous quantitative data is clearly required in order to establish this. The source of expectancies described by participants in this study were varied: some were based on hearsay, some on personal experiences, while others resulted from observations of friends or peers. It would appear that as an individual gathers more experience, their specific substance-related expectancies become more sophisticated. Additional factors are also taken into account, such as the individual's current physical or psychological state, the dosage consumed or other concurrent substance use. The majority of the sample reported positive expectancies for the drugs that they used. With the exception of alcohol, negative effects from substance use were rarely described. Where negative consequences from use were described, they were reported to have influenced future consumption patterns in an attempt to reduce the chance of subsequent negative events. Such strategies rarely involved total abstinence from substance use, but often led to changes in substance preference or patterns of use.

In our view, prevention strategies that fail to recognise the positive value that many young people place on substance use, and the functions that it fulfils for the individual, are unlikely to achieve a lasting impact on this group of young people. Nor will strategies that merely highlight the potential negative consequences from substance use. Where media campaigns were reported to have influenced consumption patterns, this may have resulted in the substitution of one psychoactive substance with another that could fulfil similar functions (such as using amphetamines instead of ecstasy).

Recommendation 6

Health messages which only stress the negative side of drug and alcohol use are in danger of being ignored by young people who already have positive experiences of

use. Instead, approaches should acknowledge the importance of the functions that drug use fulfils for some users and address possible alternative means of achieving these goals.

9.7 Availability

This is widely considered to be one of the most important contextual factors which influences whether or not someone decides to use a drug. It is the one factor that could outweigh all others in determining whether or not a substance is consumed. Our results suggest that stifling the availability of one substance may result in substituting the use of a related substance or a decision to use a different one altogether. Perhaps more worryingly, there were also reports that the lack of availability of a preferred drug had prompted initiation into the use of other, often 'harder' drug types. One example of this was using amphetamines for the first time when cannabis was unavailable. Overall, it is unclear what the public health consequences are likely to be from such selective substitution.

Recommendation 7

Education and information programmes (including campaigns) should target a range of substances that fulfil similar functions rather than single drugs in isolation and tackle the likelihood that some young people will substitute other substances. We need to adopt more sophisticated holistic responses which consider the consequences of substitution when a preferred drug is unavailable.

Prevention programmes that aim to deter all illicit substance use overlook the possibility that someone who has been using drugs heavily could substitute a licit alternative in comparable quantities, thus exposing themselves to similar (or even greater) health risks.

Recommendation 8

Education programmes should not make a division between licit and illicit psychoactive substances, as their use is clearly linked for many individuals.

9.8 Finance

The data clearly shows that, for most of this group of young people, psychoactive substances were high on their list of spending priorities. Overall, we found that the average amount spent on clothes and shoes was very similar to that spent on alcohol and other drugs. It seems that this group of young people placed an equal or greater priority on psychoactive substances relative to more essential consumer items. For most of them, the total amount spent on cigarettes, alcohol and other drugs was at least half of their monthly disposable income. Data from the qualitative interviews supported these findings, with most respondents reporting that they prioritised expenses associated with socialising over everything else. However, there was also evidence that some people had made a conscious decision to curtail their use in order to have more money available for other things. A few cannabis smokers reported that they sometimes sold small quantities of cannabis to friends in order to earn their own supply for free. In times of limited finance, they could therefore manage without having to curtail their use. In contrast to this, the use of other illicit drugs (particularly ecstasy) would often be reduced if money was short.

Recommendation 9

A possible intervention approach to target the 'finance' factor might encourage people to consider their spending priorities.

9.9 Social influences: peers and friends

When asked to describe their social circle, participants often reported that they socialised with more than one group of people. Although it was common to have close friends whose substance-using patterns were similar to their own, many also described having friends with quite different patterns of use. Some differentiated between circles of friends according to their drug or alcohol use, referring to non-drug users as their 'straight friends'. These individuals tailored their substance use according to the group norms of those with whom they were socialising. Although the data suggest that friends were definitely associated with the opportunity to use drugs, there was little evidence to support the idea of 'peer pressure'. The general opinion seemed to be that substance use was engaged in through personal choice rather than as a result of social pressures. This perhaps supports a peer-led approach to drug prevention and education as opposed to prevention programmes which try to equip young people with the skills to resist 'peer pressure'. However, such methods would need to be sophisticated in order to be effective, as the influence of peers was perceived to be only one of a range of factors, and reports of drug use when alone were not uncommon. Emphasising the functions of substance use may enable concepts such as 'peer pressure' or 'peer influence' to be acknowledged without regarding them as the major explanation for all forms of use. On the one hand, people who appear to be influenced by peer drug use could be described as using drugs with the function of helping them to feel part of a social group. On the other hand, reports of the solitary use of amphetamines by a young sales assistant who worked long hours could be explained primarily in terms of how they helped him feel more energetic and less tired.

Recommendation 10

The limitations of the current sample should not be overlooked. However, in our view, purchasers should not select local programmes that depend solely on resistance skills for users within this age group. Instead peer-led approaches could be more suitable, especially if designed to incorporate a functional approach to substance use decision-making.

9.10 Media influences

Substance-related beliefs and expectancies have been targeted through mass media campaigns, which have publicised the potential negative effects of certain forms of substance use. However, there is limited evidence that such campaigns are effective. This is particularly likely if the target audience has already used the target substance and has conflicting positive expectancies concerning its effects. Although some of our respondents cited general mass media as a major influence over their decision-making, these views tended to focus on sensationalist press coverage of ecstasy-related deaths. There was also evidence to suggest that once again this had led some simply to substitute an alternative drug (such as amphetamines) in order to fulfil the required function. Again, this emphasises the importance of considering the impact of interventions on the range of drugs that young people use rather than focusing attention solely on a single substance.

Media coverage was mainly mentioned by participants in relation to ecstasy use. Several respondents had been strongly influenced by the news stories of ecstasy-related deaths. In some cases, this had led them to conclude that the possible benefits of using this drug were not worth the attendant risks. Others had either dismissed the accounts completely, or offered explanations which cast the victims as incompetent drug users. Some had constructed certain rules for themselves, such as limiting their use or drinking sufficient liquids, which they thought would keep them safe when using ecstasy. In contrast, the lack of high profile media stories relating to amphetamine use seemed to have resulted in the deduction that this was far less dangerous than ecstasy.

9.11 Transitions

As previously noted, initial experimentation with drug use does not necessarily carry the greatest health risks. Instead, the transition into regular or excessive patterns of use is likely to carry substantially increased risks to health. The initial stages of substance use are clearly relevant to this process as they form an intrinsic part of the path followed to habitual or problematic substance use. Respondents who had used a drug on more than just an experimental basis were asked to describe what had influenced the escalations and reductions in their consumption patterns. The set of factors that emerged from the data closely resembles those identified earlier as influencing decisions concerning which substances to use. More detailed examinations of the prevalence and relative importance of each of these factor domains could be used to inform future interventions targeting novice drug users. As discussed earlier, it is important not to forget that predisposing factors external to the individual, such as social exclusion, are likely to be important in individuals' transitions to problematic drug use.

9.12 Deciding on limits for substance use

Many respondents described strategies for limiting their substance use. On some occasions, the amount used was dictated by availability, finance or some other external circumstance. There were also many reports of deliberate methods being used to limit consumption. Responses divided most people into one of two categories: those who limited their intake by dose (amount) for fear of ill-effects and those who continued to use until time or money dictated otherwise. Using time or money to limit use was a deliberate strategy for some, though for others this was by default rather than through a conscious decision. The data also suggest that an individual who used 'dose limiting' strategies for one drug might use a different strategy to limit use of another.

Recommendation 11
Educational programmes should encourage users to consider the quantities of a psychoactive substance they consume and to identify different limiting strategies.

9.13 Future research

Finally, in terms of future research priorities, we believe it would be highly valuable to quantify the schema developed in this study and to explore the key issues with a large longitudinal sample. A study that follows a cohort of young people over time could provide a valuable knowledge base for informing the development of future drug prevention initiatives. This study has highlighted four additional issues in need of further investigation:

- The role played by finances in drug and alcohol use. How the relative cost or availability of different substances affects consumer preference.
- How drugs are traded amongst young people and the impact this has on consumption patterns and availability.
- The schemata used by young people for distinguishing between acceptable and unacceptable patterns of substance use with regard to drug type, frequency of use, route of administration, negative experiences or negative behavioural correlates and how these factors are mediated by peer allegiances.
- How functions for use vary between different substance types and how these relate to patterns of substitution.

REFERENCES

Aldridge, J., Parker, H. & Measham, F. (1995) *Drugs pathways in the 1990s: adolescents' decision-making about illicit drug use*. SPARC, Department of Social Policy and Social Work, University of Manchester.

Azjen, I. (1985) 'From decisions to actions: a theory of planned behaviour', in Kuhl, J. & Beckmann, J. (eds) *Action-control: from cognition to behaviour (11–13)*. Springer, New York.

Azjen, I. (1988) *Attitudes, personality and behaviour*. Dorsey Press, Homework, IL.

Balding, J. (1996) *Young people and illegal drugs in 1996*. Schools Health Unit, University of Exeter.

Billy, J.O., Rodgers, J.L. & Udry, J.R. (1984) 'Adolescent sexual behaviour and friendship choice', *Social Forces* **62**: 653–78.

Bonito, A.J., Nurco, D.N. & Shaffer, J.W. (1976) 'The veridicality of addicts self–reports in social research', *International Journal of the Addictions* **11**: 719–24.

Boys, A., Lenton, S. & Norcross, K. (1997) 'Poly-drug use at raves by a Western Australian sample', *Drug and Alcohol Review* **16**: 227–34.

Boys, A., Marsden, J. & Griffiths, P. (1999) 'Reading between the lines: is cocaine becoming the stimulant of choice for urban youth?', *Druglink* Jan. Feb., pp. 20–3.

Boys, A., Marsden, J., Fountain, J., Griffiths, P., Stillwell, G. & Strang, J. (in press a) 'What influences young people's use of drugs? A qualitative study of decision-making', *Drugs: Education, Prevention and Policy*.

Boys, A., Marsden, J., Griffiths, P., Fountain, J., Stillwell, G. & Strang, J. (1999b) 'Substance use among young people: the relationship between perceived functions and behavioural intentions', *Addiction* **94**(7): 1043–50.

Brittain, C.V. (1963) 'Adolescent choices and parent–peer cross-pressures', *American Sociology Review* **28**: 385–91.

Buston, K., Parry-Jones, W., Livingston, M., Bogan, A. & Wood, S. (1998) 'Qualitative Research', *British Journal of Psychiatry* **172**: 197–9.

Butler, M.C., Gunderson, E.K. & Bruni, J.R. (1981) 'Motivational determinants of illicit drug use: an assessment of underlying dimensions and their relationship to behaviour', *International Journal of the Addictions* **16**(2): 243–52.

Carey, K. (1995) 'Alcohol-related expectancies predict quantity and frequency of heavy drinking among college students', *Psychology of Addictive Behaviours* **9**(4): 236–41.

Carman, R.S. (1979) 'Motivations for drug use and problematic outcomes among rural junior high school students', *Addictive Behaviours* **4**: 91–3.

Cato, B.M. (1992) 'Youth's recreation and drug sensations: is there a relationship?', *Journal of Drug Education* **22**: 293–301.

Christiansen, B.A, Smith, G.T., Roehling, P.V. & Goldman, M.S. (1989) 'Using alcohol expectancies to predict adolescent drinking behaviour after one year', *Journal of Consulting and Clinical Psychology* **57**: 93–9.

Coggans, N. & McKellar, S. (1994) 'Drug use amongst peers: peer pressure or peer preference?', *Drugs: Education, Prevention and Policy* **1**: 15–26.

Davies, J.B., Best, D.W. (1996) 'Demand Characteristics and research into drug use', *Psychology and Health* **11**, 291–99.

Ennet, S.T., Rosenbaum, D.P., Flewelling, R.L., Bieler, G.S., Rinwalt, C.L. & Bailey, S.L. (1994) 'Long-term evaluation of drug abuse resistance education', *Addictive Behaviours* **19**: 113–125.

Fergusson, D.M., Horwood, L.J. & Lynskey, M.T. (1995) 'The prevalence and risk factors associated with abusive or hazardous alcohol consumption in 16-year-olds', *Addiction* **90**: 935–46.

Fisher, L.A. & Baumann, K.E. (1988) 'Influence and selection in the friend–adolescent relationship: findings from studies of adolescent smoking and drinking', *Journal of Applied Social Psychology* **18**: 289–314.

Fountain, J., Bartlett, H., Griffiths, P., Gossop, M., Boys, A. & Strang, J. (in press) 'Why say no? Reasons given by young people for not using drugs', *Addiction Research.*

Fountain, J., Boys, A. & Griffiths, P. (1997) *Making decisions about drug use: a study of 100 young people in London.* Drug Transitions Study, National Addiction Centre, London.

Glaser, B.G. & Strauss, A.L. (1967) *The discovery of grounded theory: strategies for qualitative research.* Aldine, New York.

Glasner, B. & Loughlin, J. (1987) *Drugs in adolescent worlds: burnouts to straights.* Macmillan, London.

Goldman, M.S., Brown, S.A. & Christiansen, B.A. (1987) 'Expectancy theory: thinking about drinking', in Blane, H.T. & Leonard, K.E. (eds) *Psychological theories of drinking and alcoholism.* Guildford Press, New York, pp. 181–220.

Health Education Authority/BMRB International (1997) *Drug use in England: results of the 1995 National Drugs Campaign Survey.* HEA, London.

Health Education Authority/MORI (1992) *Tomorrow's young adults.* HEA, London.

Hurry, J. & Lloyd, C. (1997) *A follow-up evaluation of project Charlie: a life skills drug education programme for primary schools.* Central Drugs Prevention Unit, Home Office, London.

Jaffe, A.J. & Kilbey, M.M. (1994) 'The cocaine expectancy questionnaire (CEQ): construction and predictive utility', *Psychological Assessment* **6**: 18–26.

Johnston, L.D. & O'Malley, P.M. (1986) 'Why do the nation's students use drugs and alcohol? Self-reported reasons from nine national surveys', *Journal of Drug Issues* **16**: 29–66.

Johnston, L.D., O'Malley, P.M. & Bachman, J.G. (1995) *National survey results on drug use from the Monitoring the Future study, 1975–1994.* National Institute on Drug Abuse, Rockville, MD.

Kamali, K. & Steer R.A. (1976) 'Polydrug use by high-school students: involvement and correlates', *International Journal of the Addictions* **11**(2): 337–43.

Kandel, D.B. (1978a) 'Homophily, selection, and socialisation in adolescent friendships', *American Journal of Sociology* **84**: 427–36.

Kandel, D.B. (1978b) 'Similarity in real-life adolescent pairs', *Journal of Personality and Social Psychology* **36**: 306–12.

Kandel, D.B. (1985) 'On processes of peer influences in adolescent drug use: a developmental perspective', *Alcohol and Substance Abuse in Adolescents* **4**(3–4): 139–63.

Langer, L.M. & Warheit, G.J. (1992) 'The pre-adult health decision-making model: linking decision-making directedness/orientation to adolescent health related attitudes and behaviours', *Adolescence* **27**: 919–48.

Lloyd, C. (1998) 'Risk factors for problem drug use: identifying vulnerable groups', *Drugs: Education, Prevention and Policy,* **5**(3:) 217–32.

Magura, S., Freeman, R.C., Siddigi, Q. & Lipton, D.S. (1992) 'The validity of hair analysis for detecting cocaine and heroin use among addicts', *International Journal of the Addictions* **2**: 51–69.

Magura, S., Goldsmith, D., Casriel, C., Goldstein, P. & Lipton, D.S. (1987) 'The validitiy of methadone clients self reported drug use', *International Journal of the Addictions* **22**: 727–49.

Marsden, J., Gossop, M., Stewart, D., Best, D., Farrell, M., Edwards, C., Lehmann, P. & Strang, J. (1998) 'The Maudsley Addiction Profile (MAP): a brief instrument for assessing treatment outcome', *Addiction* **93**: 1857–67.

McKay, J.R., Murphy, R.T., McGuire, J., Rivinus, T.R. & Maisto, S.A. (1992) 'Incarcerated adolescents' attributions for drug and alcohol use', *Addictive Behaviours* **17**: 227–35.

Mott, J. & Mirrlees-Black, C. (1995) *Self-reported drug misuse in England and Wales: findings from the 1992 British Crime Survey.* Research and Planning Unit Paper 89. Home Office, London.

Newcomb, M.D., Chou, C-P., Bentler, P.M. & Huba, G.J. (1988) 'Cognitive motivations for drug use among adolescents: longitudinal tests of gender differences and predictors of change in drug use', *Journal of Counselling Psychology* **35**: 426–38.

Nurco, D. (1985) 'A discussion of validity', in Rouse, B.A., Kozel, N.J. & Richards, L.G. (eds) *Self report methods of estimating drug use: meeting current challenges to validity.* NIDA Research Monograph 57, pp. 4–11. National Institute on Drug Abuse, Rockville, MD.

Nurco, D.N., Balter, M.B. & Kinlock, T. (1994) 'Vulnerability to narcotic addiction: preliminary findings', *Journal of Drug Issues* **24**: 293–314.

Oetting, E.R. & Beauvais, F. (1987) 'Peer cluster theory, socialisation characteristics, and adolescent drug use: a path analysis', *Journal of Counselling Psychology* **34**: 205–13.

Oetting, E.R. & Beauvais, F. (1990) 'Adolescent drug use: findings of national and local surveys', *Journal of Consulting and Clinical Psychology* **5**: 385–94.

Ramsay, M. & Spiller, J. (1997) *Drug use declared in 1996: latest results from the British Crime Survey.* Home Office, London.

Rosenbaum, D.P., Flewelling, R.L., Bailey, S.L., Ringwalt, C.L. & Wilkinson, D.L. (1994) 'Cops in the classroom: a longitudinal evaluation of drug abuse resistance training. (DARE)', *Journal of Crime and Delinquency* **31**: 3–31.

Sebald, H. & White, B. (1980) 'Teenagers' divided reference groups: uneven alignment with parents and peers', *Adolescence* **15**: 979–84.

Stacy, A.W., Leigh, B.C. & Weingardt, K. (1994) 'Memory accessibility and association of alcohol use and its positive outcomes', *Experimental and Clinical Psychopharmacology* **2**: 269–82.

Swadi, H.S. (1992) 'Relative risk factor in detecting adolescent drug abuse', *Drug and Alcohol Dependence* **2**: 253–4.

Tolsen, J.M. & Urberg, K.A. (1993) 'Similarity between adolescent best friends', *Journal of Adolescent Research* **8**: 274–88.

Van Meter, K.M. (1990) 'Methodological and design issues: techniques for assessing the representatives of snowball samples', in Lambert, E.Y. (ed.) *The collection and interpretation of data from hidden populations*, pp. 31–3. National Institute on Drug Abuse, Rockville, MD.

Wilks, J. (1986) 'The relative importance of parents and friends in adolescent decision-making', *Journal of Youth and Adolescence* **1**: 323–34.

Zinberg, N.E. (1984) *Drug, set and setting: the basis for controlled intoxicant use.* Yale University Press, New Haven, CT.